Advance Praise for
A Mind Full of Music

"Chris Forhan can get right inside your head, because as you follow his responses to music, you'll very likely recognize yourself."

—Greil Marcus, author of *Mystery Train: Images of America in Rock and Roll Music* and *Lipstick Traces: A Secret History of the 20th Century*

"If a book can be a love song, Chris Forhan's *A Mind Full of Music* is it, and its muse is the art form itself. Chris's well-researched and deeply thoughtful observations on the songs that shaped his life are a joy to read! We were often reminded of the reasons we too were drawn to song craft and its ability to broaden our emotional spectrum, transport us through time, and teach us, again and again, something important about ourselves. This book does just that, revealing a hard-earned wisdom that both derives from and informs the music that it celebrates."

—Matty Gervais and Charity Rose Thielen, of the band
The Head and the Heart

"With the obsessiveness of a music geek and the lyricism of a poet, Chris Forhan's *A Mind Full of Music* dissects and re-assembles the bodies of songs—from the bones, blood and skin, to the brains, beating heart and soul. A spectacular deep dive into the intimate workings of this mystery we call music."

—Liz Prato, author of *Kids in America: A Gen X Reckoning* and *Volcanoes Palm Trees and Privilege: Essays on Hawai'i*

"A brilliant journey through time and the mind—a poet's road-trip with a soundtrack of popular music astutely and lovingly evoked and analyzed. Chris Forhan knows popular music through his ears, his brain, his heart—and he has the eloquence to prove it and to take us with him on this enthralling journey into song's formative power—its power to create and sustain our individual sense of self, braided as it is with strands of melody, memory, emotion, and imagination. Lucky readers us, who can't help but be encouraged by his lucid prose to undertake our own, parallel journey into the musical sources of our being. Generosity, insight, and shrewd love underlie the whole text. This is a wonderful book!"

—Gregory Orr, author of *Selected Books of the Beloved*

"I miss the days of mixtapes, friends' handwriting shining through the plastic boxes of cassette tapes they had carefully recorded. A mixtape was a deeply personal gift, one that shed great light on the person who took the time to make it, offering a window into their heart. *A Mind Full of Music* offers a similar gift. This book is a four dimensional mix tape, one full of deeply personal reflection threaded through with illuminating meditations on the power of music. I love how Chris Forhan enriches his book with sources ranging from literature to philosophy to the social sciences, all of it grounded in a deep love of music and the way it informs (and is informed by) our lives. Just like a mix tape, this book inspired me to think about the songs that have been most important to me and how, to paraphrase one of Forhan's beautiful sentences, my imagination has flooded them with private light. *A Mind Full of Music* is full of light, itself, full of charm, full of life."

—Gayle Brandeis, author of *The Art of Misdiagnosis* and *The Delta Girls*

Also by Chris Forhan

My Father Before Me: A Memoir
Ransack and Dance
Black Leapt In
The Actual Moon, the Actual Stars
Forgive Us Our Happiness
X: A Poem

Published in the United States by Overcup Press, LLC., Portland, Oregon.

"The Schuylkill," used with permission of University of Chicago Press, from JAB by Mark Halliday, 2002; permission conveyed through Copyright Clearance Center, Inc.

Excerpt(s) from SWANN'S WAY by Marcel Proust, translated by Lydia Davis, translation copyright © 2002 by Lydia Davis. Used by permission of Viking Books, an imprint of Penguin Publishing Group, a division of Penguin Random House LLC. All rights reserved.

Library of Congress Cataloging in Publication data is available.

Book design by Sean Paul Lavine of Stellr Design.
Cover design by Cole Gerst of Option-G.

Manufactured in Canada.

Overcup Press
4207 SE Woodstock Blvd. #253
Portland, Oregon 97206

ISBN: 978-1732610361

overcupbooks.com
chrisforhan.com

A Mind Full of Music

*Essays on Imagination
and Popular Song*

Chris Forhan

Contents

Track List

For my brother, Kevin,
who almost always heard it first

Part One
The Self's Song

1 | A Mind Full of Music

Each November, for Thanksgiving week, my wife, our two sons and I drive 700 miles from Indianapolis to New York. As we first pull onto the interstate—as I begin to think of our town as a separate place on the map, one we are saying goodbye to—a fragment of an old pop song enters my mind: "God didn't make little green apples / And it don't rain in Indianapolis / In the summertime."

The miles roll by. Cornfields, farmhouses, billboards, truck stops, and exit signs flash in and out of vision, but my mind attends only partially to them; it also listens to songs drifting in and out of my consciousness, a soundtrack to our travels that I can't help but sing to myself. We cross the Ohio border, Dayton beginning to appear on the mileage signs, and I imagine that town in 1903, horses clopping down unpaved streets pulling buggies, neighbors inviting each other to tea, and my mind croons, "It's a real nice way / To spend the day / In Dayton, Ohio." That Randy Newman song makes me remember another of his Ohio songs, about the burning Cuyahoga River that "goes smoking through my dreams." Other troubled Ohio tunes feel invited to crowd in: "I went back to Ohio / And my city was gone." "Four dead in O-hi-o." Eventually we cut across the tiny upraised arm of West Virginia ("almost heaven") and then into Pennsylvania, where the Clash take the stage—"Workin' hard in Harrisburg!"—and then Billy Joel—"And we're living here in Allentown." As we cross the next state line, the three Roche sisters chirp, "We come from deepest New Jersey," and then, closing in on New York City, I contemplate the impossibility, regardless of

Simon and Garfunkel's example, of counting the cars on the New Jersey Turnpike.

The city itself—after George M. Cohan and Irving Berlin and Rodgers and Hart and Ellington and Sinatra and Stevie Wonder and Lou Reed and the Rolling Stones and the Ramones and—well, the city is sunk so deep in a musical soup I could never truly see it.

Just before the Lincoln Tunnel, I mutter, "Howdy, East Orange." Dylan.

"What?" It's one of my sons, speaking up from the back seat.

"Nothing," I say. "Just a song."

Just a song—among hundreds in my mind, ready to rise up and color my experience of any moment or place. Traveling through cities and states, I travel from memory to memory, melody to melody. Music that first entered my ears in the distant past annotates the present. Perhaps we can never exist purely in the here and now—never experience it for whatever it might be outside of us. Our subjective self—memory, emotion, imagination—continually shapes our perceptions of reality. For me, and I suspect for many, that self comes with a private mental mix tape. It ensures that I will never know Broadway apart from the songs about it. I will never know the Ding an sich of Dayton.

2 | Song as a Shadowy Twin

"This Diamond Ring" by Gary Lewis & the Playboys: It is 1965, and I am five, squatting at the edge of our unpaved street, poking at the dirt with a stick, watching bugs skitter and writhe. The song is popular in this year of my life, but many other songs are, too. Why is this the record that, whenever I chance to hear it over the next fifty years, transports me to that patch of dirt, the sun hot on my neck?

A certain sound: a bed of sweet strings and a chorus of male and female background singers smoothly *doo-doo-doo*-ing and *ooh-aah-aah*-ing, as in Tommy Edwards' 1958 recording of "It's All in the Game." It's the sound of the older people of my family—grandparents, great uncles and aunts—in the early 1960s, arriving in the entryway of some home where a celebratory gathering is occurring, shedding their overcoats and hats and furs.

Neurological studies have suggested that the regions of the brain we use for perceiving are the same ones we use for remembering. Is this why my ear catches a few notes on the radio of "In the Summertime" by Mungo Jerry and suddenly I am ten again, scampering barefoot through the grass of the neighbors' backyard, glasses of iced tea on their patio table sweating beads of water? Is that why, last week, sitting at an outdoor café, I saw at a nearby table a bead of water sliding slowly down a glass, and I began humming "In the Summertime"?

✦

In his poem "Thirteen Ways of Looking at a Blackbird," Wallace Stevens distinguishes between what we hear and what our minds make of what we hear:

I do not know which to prefer,
The beauty of inflections
Or the beauty of innuendoes,
The blackbird whistling
Or just after.

The blackbird whistles; the sound waves reach our ear. The imagination, "just after," discerns—in the pitch, rhythm, and timbre—innuendoes. I am interested in those innuendoes, in how we cannot help but experience them; in how they are born of memory and chance; in how they are necessarily subjective and private, incompletely share-able; and in how they contribute to the continual making of us —which is to say, of our independent understanding of, and reaction to, the world.

Whatever we know of reality can never be situated entirely outside ourselves; because we experience the world not only through our physical senses but through our emotions and imagination, the eye and ear do not merely perceive reality but, as William Wordsworth wrote, "half create" it.

Because of this fact about us, music exists; it is made to be met halfway. The listener cannot help but respond subjectively to the music and thus does much of the work. Aaron Copland wrote of how the "beautiful" is discovered in music through "the inrushing floodlight of one's own imagination." He was referring specifically to the experience of listening to complex orchestral music, but the idea feels true, too, in relation to the music that has mattered most to me, the music I can't get out of my head: certain popular songs of the last hundred years. Why would I remember them, and remember them with such pleasure and power, if my imagination had not flooded them with a private light?

✦

When perception and memory become disjoined, when people suffering severe dementia seem to have forgotten everything, even their spouses and children, even who they themselves are, music can make them remember. Maybe that is because music integrates disparate parts of the self that might otherwise be sundered; almost every region of the brain lights up in the presence of it.

Oliver Sacks wrote of how listening to or singing songs can reawaken people with dementia to buried aspects of themselves, to entire "moods and memories, thoughts and worlds that had seemingly been completely lost." The music brings them into a mental alertness and emotional fullness they typically no longer show. It is as if song is a shadowy twin that accompanies us, an aural replica of the coherent, dynamic self we conceive ourselves as being. A piece of music is a whole, organic, living thing—complex in its shapely movement—and that fullness of being melds with the workings of our memory and thus reminds us of ourselves. A song is a message in a bottle, and the message is us.

✦

Psychiatrist Anthony Storr claimed that music is so essential to the way we perceive of reality that it is hardly possible to imagine ourselves existing without it: "Even if playing music were forbidden, and every device for reproducing music destroyed, we should still have tunes running in our heads, still be using music to order our actions and make structured sense out of the world around us."

This is what the mind does: it makes sense of things, even if the sense is necessarily a tentative and private fiction. This impulse is our "blessed rage for order," as Wallace Stevens calls it—"rage" and "blessed" being crucial adjectives: the need for order is a powerful, inherent restlessness in the mind, a fire that cannot be quenched, and there is a hint of blessedness, of divinity, in it. Of the order that we half-discover and half-impose, we construct a myth to live in.

When we make a song, when we organize sound in a new way, we give a new shape to reality, or to an experience of reality. The song is the sound of a perception. And the song itself then becomes a new reality, one to which each listener gives a private shape.

In thus stirring our imagination, music makes us alive to the present. It is, as Gaston Bachelard says of any art, "an increase of life, a sort of competition of surprises that stimulates our consciousness and keeps it from becoming somnolent." Nietzsche goes so far as to say, "Without music, life would be an error." Music exists not because it contributes to life but because it is life. This would explain why there is some music people claim not to understand.

3 | You Cannot Listen to the Same Song Twice

When our son Oliver was four, he discovered Elton John's "Crocodile Rock" and seemed to believe that for the rest of his life he would never need another song. "Play 'Crocodile Rock,'" he would say after we had climbed into the car and fastened our seat belts and were backing down the driveway. (Much of our family listening occurs when we are driving together.) One day, Oliver announced from the back seat that he wanted to hear the song ten times in a row. "Ten times?" my wife and I asked. "Are you sure?"

"Yes, ten."

"Okay."

After we'd played the song six times, Oliver announced, "That's enough. Stop."

On his third, fourth, and fifth listen, the song in his head couldn't have been exactly the same song he had first heard; what might have initially sounded goofily surprising and rollicking and melodically inventive was becoming predictable. Oliver was a different boy from the one he had been twenty minutes before; his mind was clotted with so much knowledge about the song that he could not hear it again with wide-eyed delight. As for me, Oliver's sixth hearing of "Crocodile Rock" that day might have been the 405th of my lifetime. The record was a number one hit when I was in seventh grade—for a time that year, it was part of the daily weather. In the moments when Oliver was only beginning to revel in Elton John's ludicrous leap into his high-pitched Speedy Gonzales *l-a-a-a la-la-la-la l-a-a-a*'s,

I was hearing the song through the filter of the forty years that had passed since I'd first heard it. I was simultaneously flashing on images of being thirteen—the bell-bottoms, the pizza joint jukeboxes, the beat-up Converse All-Star basketball shoes; feeling nostalgic for that lost time; accusing myself of sentimentality for feeling such nostalgia; recognizing the strange luck of sharing, with gladness, a silly song of my youth with my own young son, for whom it was new; and thinking that the song is, though a pastiche and a trifle, indisputably infectious.

Three years after asking to hear the song ten times straight, Oliver was seven and claimed still to love "Crocodile Rock" best of all Elton John songs, but his love for it had changed: it had become infused with his own nostalgia for a memorable day in his life and for a four-year-old's particular kind of outlandish obsessiveness. If we ever chance to hear the song's opening piano chords, then the insistent Farfisa organ, Oliver muses, "Remember that day I wanted to hear this all those times in a row?"

Before it reaches us, music is not yet entirely itself. It is only molecules vibrating in air; our ear—the ear drum, ossicles, cochlea, and auditory nerve—translates them into sound. In this way, only in our head does a song fully exist. And once it's there, our experience of it is colored by our imagination, whose activating agents are memory and emotion.

It is not true, then, that the song remains the same. A recording produces identical vibrations each time it is played, but we cannot hear it the same way twice. We might program our stereo or iPod or Discman to "repeat," but we cannot program ourselves to do the same.

I sometimes want to listen to a new song a second time, then a third—not just because I hope to repeat the initial pleasure I felt in hearing it but because I expect my listening will deepen and bring new pleasures. I also sometimes decide, after many listenings to a song, that I would be content not to hear it again for years, or maybe ever; I am inured to its charms. I own hundreds of CDs and vinyl LPs, collected over decades. In the mood to listen to something, I scan their spines on the shelves. Sometimes nothing catches my interest. I can't imagine listening, with pleasure, to any of these records—each of them feels distant from me, insufficient. Who bought this music, anyway?

One can never again hear a song for the first time, or the fifth or fourteenth. Any subsequent listen is informed by previous listens and by the life one has lived in the meantime. Hearing a long-cherished song recalibrates my relationship to time, both the present in which I am hearing it and the past when I first felt the song mattering to me. Listening, I feel myself connected equally to the present and to the past, or connected to the past through the present, or vice versa. The song, through repeated listenings, recovers in me what I was when I first heard it. I am who I am now and who I was then and feel therefore somehow beyond time, a sensation alternately comforting and befuddling.

Sometimes, listening to a record I know well, I wonder, "Am I even hearing this song?" Whatever is entering my ears, I am experiencing it through a scrim of associations, some of them probably unconscious ones. On the radio, I hear the Rascals' 1968 hit "People Got to Be Free," and I don't turn the dial. *I used to love this song,* I think. I listen to it with pleasure, but what is the source of that pleasure: the distinctive musical characteristics of the recording or the nostalgia I feel for the bliss upon first hearing it when I was eight? Probably both, but the two sources of joy are so intertwined as to be inextricable from one another.

In middle age, I have grown wistful with memories of my adolescent listening. That boy in his room in the 1970s, slipping a much-loved disc from its sleeve and setting it on the turntable, has been gone a long time now. I am curious what it feels like to listen to what he loved then, the music he took into himself as if it were created with him in mind, as coded message and balm: a replica in sound of his interior condition, song after song a cathartic expression of, and release from, his tangle of private feelings. In the past fifteen years or so, vinyl albums that I sold decades ago to pay for groceries have returned to my shelves, in CD form: records by Jim Croce, Cat Stevens, Supertramp, 10cc, City Boy, Procol Harum, Electric Light Orchestra. If these records were new—released only this year—I would probably not like them, or at least not find them to my taste; their sounds might strike me as formulaic, cheesy, or emotionally empty, their lyrics strained or insipid. But those records were important to me once; day by day, through junior high and high school, they helped me live my life. As I was becoming my self, they helped me sense what that self was. The contemporary philosopher Theodore Gracyk, who has a special interest in the aesthetics of popular music, observes that "musical works themselves serve as a prototype of the elusive sort of *thing* that we seek in trying to establish personal identity. Musical works offer a model of the *type* of intangible object that we seek when we seek ourselves. . . . The mere act of listening to music can be a model for finding extra-musical identity. One result is that the music that still resonates in memory and imagination can, decades later, revive experiences that are profoundly *of the self*, for they are echoes of the very experience of becoming ourselves."

He's right: forty years after my obsessive high school listening, I play an entire album by City Boy, and the songs return me to the boy I was; he has been in me and needed only the conjuring. But am I enjoying this music *now*? Yes, I think so. Still, I recognize the pleasure as secondhand: it involves the alluring bemusement of recalling a long-ago time when I could take undiluted joy in this record—even find in it instruction in how to live. In other moments, I alter my ears just a bit, and the music becomes numbskull rock, almost unlistenable. It feels one step removed from Styx. And I loathe Styx.

My nostalgic listening is always tinged with guilt, a suspicion that, in exhuming emotions I felt in a much earlier time, I am playing it safe, dallying with feelings that have died, ones that can't hurt me. But can listening to a record we loved decades ago conceivably make us feel a new emotion, not just remember an old one? Greil Marcus believes that it is possible for a recording to contain so much ambiguity, meaningful mystery, and human complexity—so much greatness, in other words—that it cannot help but remain vibrantly alive, keeping us attentive to the present. "Like a Rolling Stone" is his example: "Because the song never plays the same way twice—because whenever you hear the song you are not quite hearing a song you have heard before—it cannot carry nostalgia."

Most records are not so lucky. Certain classic rock songs I can never listen to again, not really: "Hotel California," "Stairway to Heaven," "Free Bird," "Carry On Wayward Son." There are others. When a radio station plays "Stairway to Heaven," it seems a kind of prank, an existential exercise, a test of whether a song that has been played on the radio millions of times can be experienced as dynamic, invigorating, and unfolding in the moment, as opposed to inert—as little different to the ears than eight minutes of steady humming, in the way an old beige office carpet can be walked on for years and never noticed. Once, scanning the radio dial, I happened upon the opening moment of "Stairway to Heaven"—those sparkling, plucked guitar notes—and, as an experiment, tried to listen to the whole song, truly listen to it. I attempted to rinse my imagination clean of all previous associations and preconceptions surrounding the song: my memories of how, dozens of times, in the early '70s, I had listened to it on the radio with interest, and of how, decades before this moment, I had begun to think of the song as turgid, pretentious, and witless; I tried to ignore my knowledge of the song as being one of the most played, then overplayed, rock staples ever—aired so often it had become not just a track on a band's album but a signifier of cynical, unimaginative radio programming. I tried to suppress my usual urge, upon hearing a few notes of the song, to scamper elsewhere for something to listen to.

On this day, almost to the end, I stayed with it. Once or twice I felt on the verge of hearing the song as if it were new to me, as if I were twelve again, but the sensation would fade. I couldn't make "Stairway to Heaven" exist as a thing outside myself, something separate from what my brain, over decades, had done to it.

Of course, who knows what twelve-year-old, even then, was hearing the song for the first time? Who knows what that kid was thinking?

4 | It's Personal

In the film *It's a Wonderful Life*, Mary Hatch gets mad at a record. She yanks it off the turntable and shatters it. George Bailey, the man she has adored for years, has stopped by her house to visit, but he's in a foul mood, frustrated by his sense that he'll never have the opportunity to do the one thing he has always dreamed of: escape the "crummy little town" of Bedford Falls and "see the world." What Mary has dreamed of is that she might marry George and settle down in that crummy town. George feels some affection for her, but on this day he treats her as an alien, even an enemy—the type of person who cares for things that to him are prisons: small towns; mindless, deadening jobs; and marriage. Before George enters the Hatch family's parlor, Mary, excited by his visit, arranges the setting with reminders of a night years before when they flirted in the moonlight and sang, in harmony, "Buffalo gals, won't you come out tonight." She places on an easel a drawing of George as romantic hero, lassoing the moon, then she sets the gramophone spinning with a recording of "Buffalo Gals."

It's their song, she thinks. Or it was. George, however, doesn't feel about it—about *them*—what she does. Eager to rekindle in him the passion he once briefly showed for her, Mary smiles at him meaningfully and begins to sing along with the record, and George responds, as if to a stranger, "What's the matter?" After a couple of minutes of awkward talk that boils over into rudeness, George stomps out of the house. Meanwhile, the telephone is ringing—it is Mary's tedious boyfriend calling from out of town—and she walks toward it to answer, then suddenly veers in another direction. She marches toward the gramophone, glares for a moment at the record, thrusts the tonearm aside, grabs the record, and smashes it to bits.

Mary has invested in the song her dream of a life with George. When it seems that her dream has been shattered, it makes sense for her to shatter the symbol of it.

After we had been together for fifteen years, my first wife left me for another man. That phrase, "left me for another man"—the banality of it—was part of the problem, a contribution to my anguished bafflement. How could my life, so ostensibly intricate and textured, have been reduced to a cliché? Disconsolate, unnerved, I resigned from my teaching job and moved two states away into my sister's apartment. I slept on Dana's couch and, while she was at work during the day, took long walks, read long novels, and wrote long, failed poems. I listened to music, too, but the old recordings I knew well and cherished had been made temporarily toxic for me; too many songs, even the most seemingly benign, were suddenly freighted with painful implication. I listened only to new music: the latest sardonic offering from Randy Newman was an emotionally safe favorite.

One night, my brother, Kevin, was in town, visiting from the other side of the country, and the three of us sat around the apartment eating, reminiscing, joking, drinking red wine, I drinking more than was good for me, my wont in those weeks. Throughout the evening, music played in the background. Dana chose the CDs. We drank and laughed, music murmuring and humming behind us. We talked and refilled our glasses and toasted ourselves, the reunited siblings. Sometimes we went silent for a moment, then the talk reignited. The music played. We drank and talked. "I fall to pieces . . . ," someone sang in the distance. I looked down at my glass and took a big swig. We kept talking. "Why can't I forget you / And start my life anew . . . ." It was Patsy Cline, her familiar convincing, mournful, quavering tone. "It was in the springtime / That you said goodbye . . . ."

"Take it off," I said. "Now. Get that music off." The songs were attacking me, bludgeoning me. Dana leaped up and pushed the stop button.

For twenty years, I had loved those Patsy Cline songs. Their exquisite, implacable sadness had always made me happily drop my defenses and give in to them with pleasure and empathy. But they were taunting me now, filling the room with the sounds of the excruciating thing inside me that I had been trying to escape from.

We hear what we hear: the momentary condition of our mind and heart makes a music's meaning. In 2007, I had been listening again and again to M. Ward's album *Post-War*, which I discovered only because it was sent to me, samizdat-style, by Kevin, who, throughout our decades as adults, has been in the habit of mailing me music he thinks I might like. I had never heard of M. Ward. The album felt like a powerful secret my brother had shared with me.

That summer, I felt myself falling in love with Alessandra, the woman who would give me reason to marry again. She was at the wheel of her car one afternoon, and I was poking around among the CD cases strewn on the floor. I noticed *Post-War*. "You know M. Ward?" I said.

"Love him," she replied. This was a good sign, a very good sign. Alessandra was in the tribe.

We sang along together to the CD, skipping back several times to the first track, "Poison Cup," which was, it seemed, becoming our song. "A sip or a spoonful won't do," M. Ward sang. "No, I want it all." He was saying for us what we weren't yet ready to speak out loud: that we were weary of being defensive—that we desired to surrender completely to the feelings that were overtaking us. We wanted to drink the whole cup.

A decade later, Alessandra and I had been married for years and had two young sons. When M. Ward and his band came to a small club in Bloomington, we drove down from Indianapolis for the show. Afterward, we noticed one of the musicians in his band, Scott McCaughey, lingering outside the dressing room. I walked over, and he chatted amiably with me for a couple of minutes. Then I couldn't help myself. I told him Alessandra and I were thrilled that the band had played "Poison Cup" that night since it was our song—and was, in fact, our wedding music. At the small outdoor ceremony, attended by only us, our two witnesses, and the judge, we let "Poison Cup" play over and over again, on repeat, on a portable CD player.

"Hmm," Scott said. "Kind of fatalistic, don't you think?"

"Poison Cup" was not to him what it was to us. He was thinking of the poison. We were thinking of the cup.

5 | *The Why and How of This Book*

This book contains the musings of a passionate layperson. I am neither a musician nor a music theorist, nor philosopher, psychologist, or neuroscientist; I am, instead, someone who has been listening to, and thinking about, songs his whole life. I can't get them out of my head—and don't want to—and suspect that, if my life were absent of song, my perceptions, my understanding of reality, my understanding of myself would be different. I might hardly feel I had a self at all.

My vocation is poetry; I write it, write about it, and teach it. Since my teenage years, I have fiddled with syllables, letting one word bump against another and listening to the consequences, arranging and rearranging lines in the hope of creating a meaningfully dramatic shape, a verbal music suggestive of feelings that lie just beyond language's ability to name them. That's not so different from what songs do. In fact, the genesis of my decades of devotion to poetry is a love of music. At eleven, inspired by the gift of a guitar and a beginner's guide to chords, as well as the feelings stirred within me by my fledgling record collection, I started writing songs. They were simple, lyrically and structurally, as well as—in important ways—false: they were the sound of someone trying to sound like someone who knew how to write a song. When my talent, discipline, desire, or all three faltered once too often, I set the guitar aside, let the melodies fall away, and was left with the words—and with the urge to make poems. Still, songs continued to bring life to my life, and their presence as a ghost behind my poems has not diminished. In the classroom, I find myself alluding to music as a way of thinking about poetry, and I teach an entire course on the relationship between song and literature: on how listening to a record can be both like and unlike reading words on the page.

I intend to contemplate here the dynamic interplay between recorded popular songs and us who listen to them: the way the mind makes sense of a song and the song helps the mind make sense of everything else. As someone who put his guitar away forty years ago, I will not be naming notes, chords, keys, or time signatures. As a poet and teacher of literature, I will be discussing aspects of songs that come naturally for me to talk about: structure and melody and lyric—the places a song takes us, psychologically and emotionally, measure by measure. Throughout the book, I will often use the term "song," but almost always I might as well use the word "record." I was born in the twentieth century, so my experience of music is for the most part an experience of recorded music. When a song matters to me, it is a particular recording of the song that matters. I have enjoyed symphonic and chamber music, opera, and instrumental jazz, but you will not find meaningful discussion of those genres here. For any number of reasons—some of which I will meditate upon later—I have been most deeply affected by compact songs that involve vocals, whether the tunes can be defined as inhabiting the category of rock, pop, soul, blues, jazz, folk, country or some combination of these.

When I write at some length about a recorded song, it will not be just because I am fond of the tune; it will be because it feels representative of ideas I am puzzling over. I do not intend here to list and celebrate my favorite songs— we can all do that, and it is not purpose enough for a book.

Nonetheless, the songs I have chosen to think about in these pages are ones that, at some time or another, I fell hard for, songs that have burrowed into my consciousness and nest permanently there. I would not care to write about them if I were not somehow at their mercy.

6 | *Imagining Imagining*

"CAROLINE, NO"

The Beach Boys

1966

The first time I listened to this song, I was sixteen. All I heard was its gorgeous, persuasive sorrow. I believed what the singer believes: that he is a victim, bereft and bewildered by the changes he has witnessed in his beloved. She is no longer the girl who won his devotion, so what can he do with that devotion now? I had not yet experienced the kind of love or loss the song addresses, but, with the song's help, I imagined them. I felt sad in advance.

More than forty years later, having experienced some broken relationships of my own, I still feel the song's sorrow, but I am beginning to think the singer is to blame for it. If your vision of love is idealized, and your lover—being human, thus imperfect and changing—fails to live up to it, and you suffer as a result, whose fault is that?

The song is the final one on an album, *Pet Sounds*, that begins with "Wouldn't It Be Nice," an idealistic paean to a simplistic adolescent conception of romance, which holds that all two young lovers need for pure bliss is the trading of rings: "We could be married, / And then we'd be happy." As the album progresses, it is possible to hear the subsequent songs as interrogating this initial idealism by putting the lead singer—usually Brian Wilson, who wrote most of the tunes—through various changes, relationships, and tests of character. By the time "Caroline, No" appears, the singer has come to understand that love and its consequences are more complicated than "Wouldn't It Be Nice" would have it. One might call him disillusioned. However, his innocent idealism remains. He may be living as much in illusion as ever, for the song suggests not a reconsideration of his possibly naive conception of love but merely his disappointment in his girlfriend's failure to measure up to it.

The song begins with spare percussion: three shakes of a tambourine, followed by the single thump of a large, empty water bottle—a sound that will recur throughout the track. The percussion sounds echo, suggesting spaciousness, plenty of room for feeling and wonder, which are what Brian's first lines emphasize: "Where did your long hair go? / Where is the girl I used to know?" In these questions is a mix of hard experience and a kind of headstrong innocence: the singer feels the pain of loss, but what has been taken from him—his initial conception of his "girl," signified, superficially, by the length of her hair—might not have been entirely real in the first place. The rich instrumentation backing Brian's vocals contributes to this sense of unreality. Central to the arrangement is a harpsichord; it creates a delicate elegance—not the deep, perhaps even bluesy, earthbound quality that a piano might contribute but something ethereal and wispy, a timbre suggestive more of the mind and imagination than of the body.

Throughout the song, in high, boyish tones, the singer delivers a series of pained realizations, but those realizations feel oversimplified, not much more nuanced than the "marriage equals happiness" equation presented in "Wouldn't It Be Nice": "Where is the girl I used to know?" "That's not true." "You break my heart." That latter claim appears in one of the song's most lovely moments. In the lines "Oh, Caroline, you / Break my heart," the words that end the second verse join with those that begin the bridge to unite the two sections with a single lyric idea, the melody rising dramatically at "break my heart," heightening the song's feeling of injured innocence.

As the final verse ends, the sorrowful singing ascends into a wail—"Oh, Caroline, n-o-o-o-o"—after which no more is said. No resolution is offered. No resolution seems possible. That stagnancy, that inability of the dejected lover to find his way out of his pain, is mimicked by the circling quality of the music: the instruments, joined now by bass flutes, continue to repeat the main melody line over and over as the song fades. From first note to last, the ache in the song is real and continual, the sorrow in the singer profound and believable. As the song concludes, it is even possible not to notice how, with all of the questions the singer has asked of his girlfriend about the changed nature of their love, she hasn't been given a chance to answer. The questions are rhetorical, posed by someone beholden to an impossible ideal, someone who made up his mind about her long ago.

✦

"JUST MY IMAGINATION (RUNNING AWAY WITH ME)"
The Temptations
1971

This song is as achingly beautiful as "Caroline, No"—and, to my aging ears, it has changed as much over time, and in a similar way. When it reached the top of the charts in 1971, I was eleven, and it was just another sweet love song, a promise the world was making to me of joys I was as yet too young to feel or understand. What did I know then of how desire and imagination fuse with and fuel each other, how the mind can convince itself of just about anything, especially when left alone to do its patient work in secret? I realize now that the title of this song isn't kidding. Only imagination is in operation here, and the result is enchanting. And a little creepy. I sometimes think it is my favorite song.

From the beginning, the instrumentation is delicate, dreamy, hallucinatory, with swirling strings that fade and return, fade and return, lightly tapped percussion, and softly insistent horns. The music floats, like cloud wisps, at risk of dissipating entirely. What keeps it grounded is a connection to a real human feeling, however much that feeling might arrive out of almost nothing. Eddie Kendricks, singing lead in his high, gentle tenor, tells of his enchantment with a woman whom, through his window, he sees passing every day. That is the extent of the social reality upon which his feelings are built. It is not clear that he knows even her name, let alone anything else about her. As she walks by his home each day, where is she going? Work? School? Does she have a boyfriend? Is she married? What are her interests? What matters to her? Does she have a sense of humor? To the singer, these questions seem irrelevant; from mere glimpses of her, framed by his window—as if she were in a movie repeating itself daily—he invents in his mind an entire life with her: romance, marriage, children.

He does not envision that he might one day leave his house, approach her, introduce himself, and get to know her. Instead, he leaps ahead to imagining his joy in having "a girl like her," the other Temptations entering briefly on this phrase to add exquisite harmonies and deepen its sweetness. Although it isn't clear what kind of girl she is, he is nonetheless convinced that this is a "dream come true." In the first verse, with the singer's imagination already soaring, barely tethered to the facts of the real world, all of the lines—as is true of most lines in the song—end with a long, open vowel (*by, true, me, die*). The sounds keep the words where his mind is, in air, hovering, or they turn the words themselves into air.

To his credit, the singer realizes he is merely imagining; the chorus announces as much. But that doesn't snap him back into reality. In the second verse, he is already picturing their cozy country home and the children they will raise, his bandmates offering an enraptured "Oh, ye-e-e-a-h" at the thought. This conventional scenario of romantic bliss—the house and kids—is familiar from many popular songs before this one, such as "My Man," the most famous versions of which are probably Fanny Brice's and Billie Holiday's. In the Temptations song, Kendricks dreams of a "home out in the country / With two children, maybe three." In "My Man," the singer dreams of living with her man in a "cottage by a stream" with "perhaps a kid or two." A big difference between the two fantasies, however, is that Kendricks' is entirely unmoored from reality; he has no relationship with the woman about whom he croons. The singer in "My Man" is already in a very real relationship with her man, and the song's central tension is between the intensity of her yearning for conventional happiness and the power of her man, through violence, betrayal, and disdain, to undermine it, to get "hot" and tell her "not to talk such rot." The tension in the Temptations song is elsewhere—not between a man and a woman but entirely within the man himself: between the ease with which he escapes into fantasy and his meager ability to consider reality as it is. The latter is no match for the former, so the song's appeal comes mainly from its gloriously unimpeded portrayal, and celebration, of the imagination's boundless power.

In other words, while the singer might believe he is absorbed in the girl who is the ostensible subject of his attention, he is more truly absorbed in himself. A similar phenomenon—although perhaps communicated with more stark irony—occurs in the Beatles' "Baby's in Black." John, with Paul harmonizing, sings of a woman who is mourning her dead lover. Dressed in black, she can't stop pondering her lost love. Meanwhile, John really wants to go out with her and, in a wildly unempathetic reading of the situation, can't understand why he's making no headway. She is wasting precious time on a "mistake / She has made," on this grieving that is "only a whim." John can't understand why she isn't thinking of him instead; after all, that's what he's doing.

As in the Beatles song and "Caroline, No," in "Just My Imagination" one domineering, deeply subjective consciousness—a mind fiercely attached to a single overriding ideal or desire—presents its case. The Temptations nonetheless are a group of five vocalists, and each of them contributes to this dream; each voice becomes part of the one voice, the one mind. At the start of the song's bridge, Kendricks surrenders the stage briefly to Paul Williams, whose much lower-pitched voice growls, soulfully, "Every night on my knees I pray." This seems to be not so much another person joining the conversation as another aspect of the character's consciousness revealing itself: a deep and desperate part of him that can't bear to think of losing his lover to another. He doesn't have her yet—and hasn't made the first move toward doing so—but is worried already that their relationship might go wrong.

Near the song's end, there is a hint that, without ever saying a word to the object of his devotion, he has already enjoyed and lost his love: "I've never met her but I can't forget her," he sings, offhandedly, as if she exists already only in his past. Something within this lovely song unsettles. With the woman having no clue about it, the singer has imagined an entire life with her and seems content to remain in the lush comfort of that imagining, in the false sense of necessity it offers. But what luck it is for him—and for us—that he has never met this woman. If he had, we would not have this song of pure pleasure, this single, lovely hallucination, this imaginative act uncontaminated by reality.

Any song is akin to a dream: an imaginative concoction that beckons us to neglect whatever reality we are in. In "Just My Imagination," the singer daydreams about a perfect, impossible love—a dream love. The song is a dream of a dream of a dream. Each time I hear it I'm a little surprised it's still there.

7 | *Loving a Song in Solitude*

In E. M. Forster's novel *Howards End*, the three Schlegel siblings attend a performance of Beethoven's Fifth Symphony. The three perceive the music in such different ways that they might as well be hearing different symphonies. For Helen, the music represents something unseen that her mind must bring to life—it is the soundtrack to a story she pictures in her imagination: she "can see heroes and shipwrecks in the music's flood." Margaret's imaginative response is more abstract; she "can only see the music." Tibby's response is more cerebral—his appreciation comes from knowing what the music, technically, is doing: "profoundly versed in counterpoint," he "holds the full score open on his knee . . . ."

The distinction between Tibby's mode of listening and Helen's is especially stark: it is the difference between conceiving of instrumental music as a wholly self-referential system, whose subject is itself, and thinking of it as a replica in sound of something in the physical world, outside itself. When the symphony shifts from the first movement to the second, Helen's attention wanders, since she cannot connect that new section to the imagined narrative she has imposed upon the piece. However, once the second movement ends, Helen becomes interested again, explaining to her aunt, "Now comes the wonderful movement: first of all the goblins, and then a trio of elephants dancing." Meanwhile, Tibby, who has no such images in his mind, "implore[s] the company generally to look out for the transitional passage on the drum." Helen responds, "No; look out for the part where you think you have done with the goblins and they come back."

If both Helen and Tibby are correct—if the same piece of music can evoke such competing responses—is there hope that we can ever fully understand and appreciate what someone else is hearing? And does it matter? The unavoidably private, subjective nature of our response to music may be exactly what makes us feel such fervor about certain songs or musicians; we love them for reasons rooted so deeply in our being that we could not begin to explain those reasons, maybe even to ourselves.

Some music seems to introduce us to feelings we had forgotten or never knew we had; we take such music to our heart because the heart is the part of us it speaks for.

Sometime in the mid-nineties, my brother sent me a tape of songs by a singer-songwriter from Georgia named Vic Chesnutt. I had never heard of him. One evening, walking the dogs through the neighborhood, I listened to the tape on my Walkman. I wasn't sure what I was hearing. The instrumentation was simple, often just a clunkily strummed guitar, strings sometimes buzzing, and Chesnutt's voice was peculiar: unpolished and shaky, with a southern drawl that coiled around his vowels like kudzu, making syllables multiply—he pronounced *attitude* as *ay-uh-ti-tyoo-ude* and *bug* as *buh-ooh-uh-ug*. His phrasing was unpredictable; some words he would sing as if in slow motion, and others he would scurry through. He seemed to be singing of subjects and angles of perception usually neglected by songwriters, conveying them through a curious tangle of Latinate and Germanic diction, words I didn't remember having encountered before in songs: *ingratiations, gumption, triangulating, oozing, convex, noggin, machinations, skedaddle.* He sang of being an atheist, of dancing in a dream with Isadora Duncan, of catching a kitten in a trap when he'd hoped to catch a rabbit. He called Hemingway, not inaccurately, an "articulate dead fisherman." He was conversationally direct about his internal tumult, singing, "Just a general freak that is a-boiling in me / And I'm terrified what it's a-gonna dislodge," and, "A friend of ours told me that I was disgusting."

He sounded like someone who had journeyed into a nightmare and made it only halfway back again, singing from a point between waking and dreaming, between this world and some other nameless one hiding within it.

The songs, though incompletely engaging, were weird enough that I knew to keep listening. On perhaps my seventh time playing the tape, I got it; I locked in; the songs entered me to stay. They seemed suddenly the best expression I had yet encountered of my own muddled interior. I wondered if I could ever find meaningful pleasure again in listening to anyone else's songs.

This type of imaginative and emotional union with music had happened before to me, as it happens to many. Jonathan Lethem has written of how, at sixteen, he felt just such a connection to the third album by Talking Heads: "At the peak, in 1980 or 1981, my identification was so complete that I might have wished to wear the album *Fear of Music* in place of my head so as to be more clearly seen by those around me." During those years, I would have said the same about my head and Elvis Costello's *My Aim Is True*. Had Lethem and I, strangers to each other, passed on the street, we might have nodded to each other knowingly.

An obsession of this kind brooks no dissent. Years ago, as a teacher of college writing, I told my first-year students that they could write their essays on any subject of their choosing, just as long as it was something they deeply and genuinely cared about. A student might write first about his estrangement from a high school friend, then about his interest in mechanical engineering, then about his wavering religious faith, then about his growing understanding of his mother's plight as a single parent. Once, in 1990, a student wrote all five of her essays on New Kids on the Block, a popular boy band. As the semester progressed, a couple of times I checked in with her, inquiring whether she really wanted to write only about this band. "Yes," she said. "They are all I care about."

For a time in the nineties, the only music I cared about was Vic Chesnutt's. I became evangelical, foisting him upon friends. Some of them heard what I heard, but sometimes I was the true believer, Bible in hand, going house to house and watching door after door close emphatically in my face. When a writer friend and I drove eight hours together to a conference in Washington, D.C., I took the opportunity of the long journey to introduce him to Chesnutt. In the blindness of my faith, I played Chesnutt's music for three hours, not giving my polite listener in the passenger seat a respite. Finally, my friend said that he'd had enough and craved some music of his own; he ejected my tape and slipped in a cassette of the cast recording of *Phantom of the Opera*. Around the same time, I gave my sister a Chesnutt record for Christmas. She opened it, and we sat and listened to it together, all the way through. As song gave way to song, I cherished the gift of being witness to her first hearing of this startling, life-changing music. The final track ended. Turning to me, with an expression both exhausted and apologetic, she said, "I sort of hated it."

It is a kind of loneliness, loving a record in solitude. The music speaks to me—seems even to speak *of* me—and I yearn to respond. But to whom? The musician? I have lingered in parking lots after Elvis Costello concerts in order to say something, anything, to the man whose songs helped me survive my late teens. When I was nineteen, I asked for his autograph, and he obliged. In later years, I mentioned to him being surprised by a song he had played that night, or I complimented his guitar playing, or I asked for a photo with him, or I handed him a book of poems I had written—which he took graciously—that contains a mention of his first album.

On Christmas Day, 2009, Vic Chesnutt died. Earlier that year, I had mailed to him the same book I gave Costello, which also alludes to a Chesnutt song. Each time I published a book, I had sent it to him, with a note about my continuing thanks for his music. But I could not communicate to Chesnutt or Costello what I yearned to: what their songs had done for me—or to me. Even if I had, they might not have understood, or even cared to. After all, the meaning their music held for me was mine alone; it was born and lived entirely within me. I could not share it, not with my friends, not even with those who had written the songs. It was the songs themselves I should have been talking back to, but they don't listen: they leave us alone with our listening, in a sometimes sublime, sometimes disheartening privacy—something Mark Halliday contemplates in his poem "The Schuylkill":

Deep deep in December
driving the icy Schuylkill Expressway at 1:05 A.M.
I might have been really beautiful
as I listened to Dylan sing "He Was a Friend of Mine"
beautiful in how I understood it
but no one (the world) will ever know this—
the Schuylkill just let my beauty atomize like nothing
through the dark shadow-panes of one small black car—

there is something wrong with the whole setup.

I, too, have sensed this wrongness. In certain moments of being alone with a song, I have felt as profoundly alive as ever: as intensely attuned to what is true, as richly human. I have known a song wholly, and it has known me. I have been beautiful, for instance, in my understanding of Vic Chesnutt's "Stupid Preoccupations"—at least as beautiful, I suspect, as Mark Halliday in his understanding of Dylan. He'll just have to take my word for it.

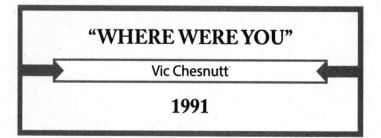

"WHERE WERE YOU"

Vic Chesnutt

1991

A couple of guitar strums, then a rest. That's how it starts. Then another strum of the same chord, a rest, and two more strums. Then another rest, two strums, another rest, two strums. Is this even a song? Is this someone just testing whether his guitar is in tune or figuring out whether he likes the sound of that one chord? Then he hits a new note, drums and bass kick in, and suddenly we're in a song, solidly so— one that will take us through the most familiar of structures: a series of verses, each leading to a chorus, with a bridge halfway through. However, as foreshadowed by that off-kilter instrumental opening, packed within that comfortably predictable structure will be a whole lot of weirdness.

Many Chesnutt songs are like this one turned inside out, disorderly in structure yet, in image or tone, unified: hallucinatory cracked southern gothic symbolist musings. This song, however, if you squint, seems as tidy and uniform a lyric as any by Irving Berlin, Ira Gershwin, or Hoagy

Carmichael. The questioning title, "Where Were You," fits neatly alongside those of any number of pop standards: "What'll I Do?" "How About You?" "Am I Blue?" Each of the four verses begins with an identical rhetorical strategy, posing a question, "Where were you," and following those three words with the identification of a moment in time, moving, as the verses progress, through a strict chronology from past to present: "Where were you two years ago," then "two weeks ago," then "last Monday," then "this Sunday." The question asked in the chorus—"Where were you, girl, / When I needed you?"—is so unembellished and earnest as to encroach on the emptily formulaic.

In all these ways, the song offers the comforts of predictability; it is balanced and symmetrical, an airtight rectangular box. But the contents of that box are alternately cryptic and funny, heart-wrenching and droll—so peculiar and personal that no one but Vic Chesnutt could have written this song.

"Where were you," the singer begins. We're eavesdropping on a private conversation—or dramatic monologue—meant for only the "you" to understand. This must be so, since he refers to things that seem entirely private: being "locked out there at the barn" and being done in by the charms of "some certain Athens sacred monster." Chesnutt lived in Athens, Georgia, so that reference is clear, but the rest is murky; the details of this tale are, it seems, for only him and her to understand. Halfway through this first verse, a cello and violin played pizzicato enter, and they will remain throughout the song, sprinkles of sweetness that serve as a foil for the singer's bitterness. (About this sonic detail, Chesnutt once commented, "Pizzicato strings on my nasty little song—I love it.")

Then the chorus arrives. "Where were you, girl, / When I needed you," the singer asks, stretching out the word "I" to four syllables and "you" to three, keeping our full attention on the two parties to this dispute. It is he—at least from his perspective—who is the injured one, and, as he lingers over the personal pronoun "I," the instrumentation drops completely away, so the word, elongated and alone, is all we hear, a tinge of self-pity in it.

There is also, however, self-awareness in the lyric, an instinct in the singer to distance himself, for an instant, from his misery and allow a hint of absurdity to enter. We hear this in the wryly impersonal quality of the diction, as when he refers to the restaurant where his erstwhile lover works in the way a governmental form might define it: it is her "place of employment." He allows himself to play the clown, moping in the restaurant—so conspicuously that another customer is compelled to inform him, "Boy, you're looking bad"—and "crying in [his] hummus." In the midst of this disconsolate narrative, the surprising appearance of mashed chickpeas gives the scene a whiff of the ridiculous, a sense intensified by the word "hummus" being given pride of place at the end of a line, as the rhyme for the previous mention of the girlfriend's mysterious, and seemingly broken, "promise."

A little rustle on the drums shifts us into the bridge, in which the singer interrupts his recounting of his suffering to speculate about what his beloved has been up to. He can't help but imagine her with another man, and he knows just where they would have met: "Were you in that second story / Well-lighted place?" This is not an abstraction—a vague guess or stock pop song phrase with generic connotations. He visualizes with painful exactness the location of her infidelity, as well as her actions and with whom she performs them: he pictures her "up against its occupant artist / In his personal space."

As with the previous "place of employment," the phrases "occupant artist" and "personal space" color this acutely personal complaint with dispassionate, hackneyed jargon, as if, to prevent a plunge into complete despair, the singer is half making fun of the situation, or himself, or her, or maybe everything; he can approach a vision of the imagined betrayal only with the protective armor of linguistic playfulness and philosophical aloofness.

The phrase "well-lighted place" does interesting double duty. It continues the vivid realism introduced in the earlier restaurant scene—this song is about actual people in actual places, not stock figures who might populate a hundred other sad love songs. It suggests that the singer has previously seen with clarity his lover well lit in that second-story setting, and, if this space is the artist's studio, we would indeed expect it to have good lighting. However, the phrase is also an allusion to Hemingway, whose story "A Clean, Well-Lighted Place" presents such a setting as a source of temporary refuge from existential emptiness; the singer might secretly understand the appeal for his lover of escaping there. He might envy her for it.

As the song continues, so do the idiosyncratic references and word choices. Another Athens allusion appears—to the 40 Watt Club, a venue where Chesnutt often played. Describing an evening of solitary drinking, he reports, paradoxically and slyly, "I was alone with Pepe Lopez" (not a person: a brand of tequila). He explains, "I just couldn't do the schmooze," the "e-e-w" vowel sound of "do" and "schmooze" elongated, making the phrase drip with dejection and disdain.

In the fourth and final verse, the singer's helplessness and self-abasement reach their peak—or nadir—in the announcement that he is "in the backyard leaking / On the spot where you proclaimed yourself." Otherwise powerless to alter his circumstance, he can at least defile the patch of ground where his faithless lover made her promise to him.

With its tale of romance gone wrong, its sweetly melancholy melody and pretty strings, and its classically repetitive structure, "Where Were You" has much in common with the tunes of the Great American Songbook. Still, its chances of becoming a standard seem slim. Irving Berlin, I would wager, in a song's climactic moment, never called upon his lovelorn hero to piss in the yard.

8 | *Song and the Deep, Unbroken Self*

It sometimes happens that a shard of song, a few bars of melody broken off the whole, will stick in my mind—haunt me for hours—but not reveal its source. I recognize the fragment but can't attach it to a complete melody, let alone recall a word of the lyrics or the musician who recorded it.

I play the series of notes over and over in my mind, listening intently for clues, keeping myself open to possibility—the song could be by anyone, and from any time—and hoping that the battering ram of repetition and rhythmic momentum will topple the wall between the phrase I am humming and whatever comes after it. The "tip of the tongue" phenomenon comes into play: I can't name the song, but I feel on the verge of being able to do so. I have some sense of a category into which the song might fit. It feels, for instance, like a big band tune—something thumping. Count Basie? Or it feels like a song from the early '70s, something intimate and earnest. Maybe James Taylor? Joni Mitchell? It's not a love song; I'm almost positive it's not a love song. It feels political, maybe environmental. "Big Yellow Taxi"? No, it's slower than that. I'm getting close. The singer, I'm thinking, has a high, reedy sound. "Well, I dreamed I saw—." Neil Young! "After the Gold Rush." The wall falls; the whole song, from beginning to end, flows unimpeded through my mind.

Once I spent most of a day with such a fragment of song nagging at me. It seemed to be a song I knew well, one I had listened to dozens of times. It felt vaguely folksy. Its instrumentation, I was willing to bet, was entirely acoustic. Probably a woman sang it. As one hour gave way to the next, the sequence of notes played on the surface of my consciousness, impish and mysterious, refusing to give up its secret. Finally, in midafternoon, I admitted defeat and called off the search. I willed myself to think of something, anything, other than that tune.

Later, as my girlfriend and I were readying ourselves to drive to a restaurant, it crossed my mind that it had been a long time—years—since I had listened to Ed's Redeeming Qualities, a quirky, literate, happily rough-hewn band, one of whose members was an old graduate school acquaintance. My girlfriend said she wasn't familiar with the group, but I was thinking one song of theirs might especially appeal to her, so, as we drove to dinner, I slid a cassette into the tape deck and pushed play. There it was: the song that had haunted me. My mind had been waiting patiently to give me the answer. I just had to stop thinking so hard.

Paul McCartney's mind gave him a tune once, when he was sleeping. He woke with a melody in his head and an exasperating inability to identify the song: its name, its author, the lyrics, if there were any. He played the tune for the other Beatles, and they didn't recognize it, nor did any other musicians he shared it with, so McCartney claimed the song as his own, tentatively named it "Scrambled Eggs," and eventually changed its title to "Yesterday." For most of us, the murky depths of the unconscious send up a nagging snippet of melody we've heard many times but now can't quite identify; only someone like Paul McCartney can't figure out where the tune came from because, without knowing it, he wrote it himself.

Billy Joel and James Taylor, too, have said that dreams have given them songs. Stravinsky claimed that he dreamed the idea for *The Rite of Spring*. The tradition of a composer feeling like a vessel through which music passes is a long one. The Venerable Bede tells the story of Cædmon, a seventh-century illiterate, unmusical Anglo-Saxon cowherd. At feast time, when the revelers decided to take turns singing, Cædmon was so certain of his lack of musical ability that, as soon as he saw the harp coming close to his place, he rose and fled for home. Alone in the cattle shed, he dozed off and dreamed of an unidentified "someone" standing by his side, instructing him to sing. Cædmon demurred, explaining that he had not the skill, but the mysterious visitor, unmoved, commanded him to sing "about the Creation." Cædmon did so; when he awoke, he remembered his dream, and he kept on singing.

Who is the "someone" who coaxed music out of Cædmon? An angel or some other emissary of God? His identity seems not to matter as much as that he appeared only when Cædmon slept. With the conscious mind at rest, some other, deeper part of us—a part liberated from fear and anxiety—is released into speech, or song. It is a realm within us beyond thought, as music is, and shares its language: wordless, abstract, free, flowing, whole.

9 | Child's Play

In his early months in the world, our son Oliver developed the habit of singing himself to sleep. Drifting toward slumber, he would begin to burble, shaping sounds noticeably musical in nature, involving shifts of pitch and rhythmic riffs. Trying a new sound, listening to it, then trying another, he seemed to be having a great time. He could not yet talk or walk, but he had music in him and the impulse to turn to it in moments of ease.

At the same time our older son, Milo, was two and toddling around the house all day gripping a tiny ukulele. He strummed and mumbled, mumbled and strummed; it came naturally to him to perform an intermittent, extemporaneous soundtrack to his activities. Soon he began writing actual songs: brief ones, but songs nonetheless. In a video clip, he sits, in diaper and T-shirt, on the living room carpet, legs outstretched, strumming ferociously and singing his first composition, titled "Fire Engine and Fire Truck." The song was inspired by his enthusiasm for fire engines and fire trucks, and it goes like this: "fire engine and fire truck."

At three, Milo created a band that he called Throw Stuff. He recruited his little brother, as well as a musically minded babysitter. Milo and Oliver wrote several tunes that arose, organically, out of their interests and concerns: a giddy song about maple syrup; a band anthem in which they snarled, Johnny Rotten-like, "Throw stuff!"; and a lament that began, "Why is everybody telling me to go to the bathroom? / I'm a big boy and I can decide when I want to." At two, three, and four, Oliver was still erupting frequently into song and was enchanted by the sounds of any instrument he could get his hands on: ukulele, guitar, drums, piano. He invented his own instruments, such as when he wrapped rubber bands around an empty, dented plastic bottle. "Look, Dad. Any place I pluck, it makes a different sound!"

Nobody had to persuade Milo and Oliver to do any of this; music was in them from the start, as it perhaps is in all of us as soon as we arrive in this world. We have an early impulse to make musical noises in order to express ourselves or, maybe more importantly, to *experience* ourselves, as a being in a body. When asked once what songs can do that prose on the page cannot, John Darnielle, who writes both songs and novels, responded, "Where does music enter? It goes into your body. So does reading, through your eyes, but it's not the same as a sound wave that literally hits a drum inside your ear, which vibrates at a frequency that then sends a message to your brain. So it's a physical experience. It's primal, and everyone has it. Infants have music."

In fact, babies might be the originators of all that we define as music. "One theory," psychiatrist Anthony Storr notes, "is that music developed from the lalling of infants. All infants babble, even if they are born deaf or blind. During the first year of life, babbling includes tones as well as approximations to words: the precursors of music and language cannot be separated."

Researchers have discovered that the impromptu making of music in a variety of forms is central to children's lives and that, for them, to sing is to solidify a sense of their separate identity. As toddlers, Milo and Oliver both were prone to emptying the kitchen cabinets of pots and pans, arranging them on the floor into a makeshift drum set, and then, with a wooden spoon, metal whisk, or plastic spatula, tapping, pounding, and clanging, as if to announce, "Here I am," as if to search for sounds that would extend outward into the sensory world some elemental rhythm or feeling they harbored within them.

We bring music into the world, and the world sings back. As we grow older, and hear more and more music, navigating through the social world involves learning which music we care about and which we could do without. Deciding what we like, we decide who we are, or would like to be. By the time he was seven, Oliver had listened to a lot of music. To his parents' delight, and with their encouragement, he had spent his early years listening almost daily to the Beatles. He loved the movie *School of Rock*, whose raggedly charming protagonist is a fan of Led Zeppelin—as, it turns out, was one of Oliver's new friends at school. He had even, at five, seen Bob Dylan live, joining his parents and brother for a summer lawn concert that ran deep into the evening, causing him mainly to lie weary in the grass, surrounded by smoking, drinking, increasingly loudmouthed and loopy adults, Dylan on a far stage talk-singing raspily amid a muddy mix.

One day, Oliver's second-grade teacher asked him to write a haiku. The poem he came up with revealed that he had traveled far from the wordless infant who slid into spontaneous, unselfconscious music-making; it revealed that he was well into the process of socialization—his own inherent love of music compounded now with the influence of others' judgments and with his need to plant the flag of his opinion, to claim space in the world by defining his taste. He titled the poem "Rock":

Led Zeppelin is cool
The Beatles are very cool
Bob Dylan is dumb

Part Two
The Song in the World

10 | *Songs in Time*

In the summer of 1970, when I was ten, I came into possession of my first radio, a cheap, plastic beige transistor not much bigger than a pack of cards. I began to listen to it every chance I got. I carried it with me outside to listen while I knelt in the dirt, flattening the garden soil into little roads for my Matchbox toy cars to motor over. I hung the radio from my bicycle's handlebar and listened while I pedaled up and down the street. At bedtime, in the dark, I positioned the radio on the pillow beside my head, turning the volume low so my parents couldn't hear it.

It did not occur to me to tune in to anything but Seattle's most popular Top 40 AM station; I might not even have been aware of alternatives—classical or country or jazz stations or the weird low-wattage end-of-the-FM-dial countercultural affair staffed by earnest amateurs. Instead, the sounds that slipped through the narrow plastic bars that covered my radio's speaker were the pop songs of that summer: Clarence Carter's "Patches," Anne Murray's "Snowbird," and Freda Payne's "Band of Gold," existing for me in the way that air and water did. They seemed part of the weather, something that would always be there. With no meaningful personal history of such listening, I did not hear the songs as ephemeral—as having once not existed and as even then preparing to slip down the charts and off radio playlists to be replaced by other equally ephemeral tunes. When the station played an oldie—something, say, from two years before, from 1968, maybe "Young Girl" by Gary Puckett and the Union Gap or "Green Tambourine" by the Lemon Pipers—the song sounded ancient, disconnected from my own life: it was what people listened to in the olden days. I had no complex temporal context within which to place such a record, so it might as well have been from the big band era.

✦

That's the era, I came later to understand, that gave sustenance to my grandfather's musical imagination. He was born just before the First World War, began seriously to listen to music in the 1920s, and spent his young adulthood, his happy bachelor years, invigorated by the swinging, virtuosic sounds of Benny Goodman, Louis Armstrong, Harry James, Count Basie, and the Dorsey brothers. Fifty years after that time, my grandfather—deep into retirement, his gray hair thinning, a hearing aid hooked around his ear—still listened to, and thought about, music as he did when he was in his twenties. When my brother, a nascent jazz enthusiast, asked him how he felt about bebop, the experimental jazz—angular, inward, tense, rhythmically unpredictable—that had begun to develop forty years before, my grandfather said, "Oh, I don't like that new stuff they're doing now."

✦

It's relative, our sense of a particular music's age—and of our own. After a few years in the early 1970s listening to Top 40 radio, I turned my attention to the FM dial, as well as to records and musicians I was reading about but not necessarily hearing on the radio. The hits didn't matter so much to me anymore. I even began to feel a vague contempt for them—such disdain was part of my adolescent development, my defining of myself within, and against, the culture. In 1970, if I heard a two-year-old song, it seemed ancient. Now, in my sixties, if I hear a song from 1974—something released five decades ago—it sounds almost new. It might even strike me as representing a recent decline in the quality of popular music; that's because I associate it with a time when I began to listen to such music with a more critical ear and thus with waning interest. I was changing more than music was. Why else would I blame 1974 for Paul Anka's "(You're) Having My Baby" but hold no such grudge against 1971 for Donny Osmond's "Go Away Little Girl," which I at one time listened to willingly, eagerly, uncritically, unironically, over and over again, merely because it was on the radio?

11 | *The Pop-Rotted Mind*

Theodor Adorno thought lovers of popular music were chumps.

The music is merchandise, he argued—the songs undistinguished, nearly interchangeable products of an impersonal capitalistic machine intent on draining us of our money and, in order to do so, of our imagination and will. The dastardly secret, the mischievous trick, is that the machine keeps working by persuading us our imaginations and will are in charge. There are slight differences among songs, so we are moved by one tune more than by another; we have personal favorites and therefore, we believe, personal taste. But, Adorno wrote, pop songs are standardized and predictable and thus seductive without being particularly challenging; instead of engaging our minds, they lull us into complacency and docility. We hear a song again and again and come to like it not necessarily because of its inherent quality but because of its familiarity; we "become enraptured with the inescapable." For Adorno, to like a song "is almost the same thing as to recognize it." The trough from which we eat is filled with food we believe we have chosen, when it has instead been chosen for us. Our taste is formed for us and continually confirmed by the songs we are fed, which are similar enough for them to go down easily, without our complaining or questioning why we are bellying up to this particular trough to begin with.

Adorno had a point. When I first started listening to popular music on the radio, why did I have little sense that there was any other kind of music worth listening to? Who had told me that? Probably no one—or everyone and everything: my older sisters, with their Beatles and Dave Clark Five and Sonny & Cher records; the cars parked by the lakeside in summer, windows down, the sounds of some new hit by the Grass Roots or the Guess Who wafting from their dashboard speakers; the racks of pop 45 singles displayed at the Bartell drugstore. What did it mean for me to "like" one of those singles—built to be a hit, seducing me with its tender sentiment and catchy hook—when, I can hear more clearly now, it had evident weaknesses lyrically and musically, maybe so many that the song was kind of dumb? Often placing their bets on a record because it sounded like others that had already hit it big, record company executives, promoters, distributors, and radio-station music and program directors navigated the song into the marketplace, and I consumed it. Among the tunes on Top 40 radio in the early 1970s, I always had a favorite, but what did it mean, exactly, to prefer the Chi-Lites' "Have You Seen Her?" to David Cassidy's "Cherish," when the reason to compare them was merely that they were among several dozen recent songs that had happened to find their way onto radio playlists and therefore into my ear? In the first week of 1972, the same Top 40 charts that contained those songs also featured two versions of "I'd Like to Teach the World to Sing (In Perfect Harmony)," a tune that had initially wheedled its way into the cultural consciousness as the jingle for a Coke commercial. Perhaps its being a hit revealed not just how appealing the song was but how greatly Americans enjoyed drinking soda or watching television, or how few viewers then owned remote controls that could mute commercials with a click.

Every Sunday evening during this time, I listened to *American Top 40*, the national syndicated survey countdown show hosted by Casey Kasem that followed the weekly rankings published by *Billboard* magazine. Which songs were up, which were down, and, especially, which song was number one—these facts mattered to me. At eleven, twelve, and thirteen, beginning to feel the power of music in my life, I accepted this list unquestionably as my paradigm for determining the quality of music and for defining my own tastes. I had not yet begun to question whether the number of times a record was played on the radio or bought in stores might be only tenuously related to its aesthetic value. A popular song was a good song; if it was extremely popular, it was extremely good.

If a record reached the very top of the charts, I understood that to mean that it was of a different order than any other, even a tune just behind it at number two. A number one song was an instant classic; it had earned the timelessness granted by universal approbation. This wobbly postulate led, occasionally, to bemusement when I noticed my ears and the charts being in jarring disharmony. For instance, when I was in sixth grade, the first few times I heard Melanie's "Brand New Key," I found the record's novelty charming: the simple, tinkling piano notes, the *plunk plunk plunk plunk* rhythm, and the little-girl voice rising abruptly, playfully in pitch in the chorus. But then, as novelties do, it wore off; what I had first considered endearing I soon— and permanently—found irritating. Consequently, when the song reached number one and stayed there for several weeks, I was compelled to question my taste. Had I been unfair to "Brand New Key"? Should I like it more? (Was there perhaps some meaning I was missing in the singer's yearning for someone to insert his key into her untested roller skates?)

Sometimes a song I was passionate about didn't do well on the charts. Was Frank Mills' "Love Me, Love Me Love" less gorgeously, heart-wrenchingly sad than I thought, since it hadn't managed even to sneak its way onto the Top 40? If my current favorite song rose only to number 33 and then dropped off the list completely, part of me questioned my musical judgment, and another part wondered, of the music listeners of America, "What's wrong with these people?"

But I was these people. We were all milling about the same brightly lit showroom filled with glittering merchandise, the blinds drawn so we wouldn't suspect there was more world outside.

When I occasionally caught a glimpse of that world, I couldn't completely absorb the fact of its existence. In seventh grade, when every week I was adding to my record collection a new 45 by Three Dog Night, Elton John, Carly Simon, Neil Diamond, or Bread, I discovered that a classmate was a fan of contemporary country music. It was all he listened to. I had no place to put this information. He was a thirteen-year-old white boy from north Seattle, as I was. Who could have raised him, and insulated him so perversely, that his preferred radio station, though only an inch to the right of mine on the AM dial, played a music so unfamiliar to me that it might as well have been Neptunian? Once, returning home from a junior high field trip, my best friend and I found ourselves in the car of our journalism teacher, a gracious and elegant late-middle-aged woman who we discovered liked to listen to the radio while she drove. Her preference: the classical station. As we sat listening to oboes tweedle, cellos moan, and tympanis thunder, my friend and I didn't know what to do with ourselves. We hadn't a capacity merely to listen to, let alone enjoy, the music. Instead, we did what we were good at: suppress, just barely, our perplexed giggles.

Country and classical music were absent from my life not because I had given them a serious listen and judged them wanting; I ignored them—and other genres of music—because the cultural tributary I had from the start found myself floating on was pleasant enough to make me think it was everything, make me believe it was the only river around. Enjoying the view, unaware that beyond the horizon were other views just as beautiful, maybe more so, I was becoming Jean-Paul Sartre's imagined fan of popular music, someone who, lacking self-determination, is hardly someone at all: "If he listens to the radio every Saturday and if he can afford to buy every week's No. 1 record, he will end up with the record collection of the Other, that is to say, the collection of no one. . . . Ultimately, the record collection which is no one's becomes indistinguishable from everyone's collection—though without ceasing to be no one's."

At various times over the last sixty years, it might have seemed that every American's collection included the same record, as if it were government-issued, appearing on the doorstep unannounced, like the phone book. Why did millions of homes contain a copy of the cast recording of *My Fair Lady* or the soundtrack of *The Sound of Music* or *Sgt. Pepper's Lonely Hearts Club Band* or *Thriller* or *Their Greatest Hits* by the Eagles? Something more than mere musical quality had to have been at work: some melding of cultural, social, and commercial forces that fed each other. Danny Goldberg, who has worked in the music business since the 1960s, notes that a record "is on the chart because it's popular, and it's not just double-talk to say that it's popular, to some extent, because it's on the chart." Of my plunking cash onto the counter, during my teenage years, for my copy of *The Dark Side of the Moon* or *Frampton Comes Alive!* or *Rumours*, I wonder whether I was following my heart or following orders.

Adorno and Sartre might say the latter, and it would be hard to argue with them. In any given moment of any year of any decade, as we exist within a culture whose traits are so inescapable that they can seem invisible, like oxygen, we might listen to a popular song and think of it merely as music. Zooming out, however, and thinking of the song as part of a years-long era of popular music, we can hear how it is a product of its time—*product* not merely in being a creation of the time but in being a commodity deliberately arranged and shaped with the design to seduce listeners into paying attention to it and paying for it. What has sold before might well sell again, so the new song offered for consumption this month often sounds much like last month's hit. Would Conway Twitty's 1958 record "It's Only Make Believe" have soared to the top of the charts if Twitty hadn't tried to sound exactly like the best-selling singer of the time, Elvis Presley? Would Simon and Garfunkel's acoustic—and, originally, anemically selling—recording of "The Sounds of Silence" have found such an enthusiastic audience had it not been remixed and overdubbed by producer Tom Wilson with the same rock instrumentation, Hammond organ and all, that he had used on Bob Dylan's "Like a Rolling Stone," a surprise hit of the previous summer? Would the Motown label have landed scores of songs on the charts throughout the 1960s if it hadn't found a winning formula—the soulful yet poppy, propulsive yet melodic, explosive yet compact "Motown sound"—then stuck with it? Was it an accident that established rockers Rod Stewart and the Rolling Stones, as well as the pop-punk band Blondie, Electric Light Orchestra, and even Paul McCartney had some of their biggest hits of the 1970s with records that fit neatly into the disco playlists of the time? Is it an accident that for much of the 1980s the sounds of synthesizers and bossy, thoughtless snare drums were everywhere, like cream cheese spread from one end of the pop charts to the other?

There are good reasons to feel suspicious of formulas, to be wary of a record that seems intent on penetrating our hearts and nervous systems by taking a shortcut, a sonic path already well-worn by music that has preceded it. There are good reasons to consider how much our interest in a song is a response to its genuine impact on our imagination and how much is a response to marketing forces that have made the song impossible to ignore.

Still, every time I hear the power-pop chords, high harmonies, and hand claps of Badfinger's "No Matter What," I am defenseless against them and deliriously happy, even if the Beatles brought water from that well many times before. Certain moments in popular songs matter as much to me as any Faulkner novel or Vermeer interior or Wagner aria: the rapid tumble of drums and David Ruffin's anguished "I *know* you wanna leave me" at the start of "Ain't Too Proud to Beg" by the Temptations; the twenty-five seconds of guitarist Elliott Randall soloing, stealing the show, in the middle of Steely Dan's "Reelin' in the Years"; Gladys Knight's distraught descent through the notes of "There can be no way, there can be no way" in "Neither One of Us"; and XTC's winningly self-deprecating love song "The Mayor of Simpleton"—especially, among all of the singer's claims of his paltry intellectual power, the witty admission, "I don't know how many pounds make up a ton / Of all the Nobel Prizes that I've never won."

I would have to work impossibly hard, would have to defer to tidy theory over messy experience, would have to deny the mind my life has given me in order to repudiate such moments, to deny what they make me feel, for which I have no better word than joy.

12 | *Listening with Eyes Open*

When I was nine, a friend from up the street told me he had something I had to listen to. In his basement rec room, he showed me a 45 that his big brother had brought home; the label was orange, the song's title "In the Year 2525 (Exordium & Terminus)." My friend set the record on the turntable, then the needle in the groove, and the sound—tense, trembling strings, an annunciatory horn, portentous vocals—spooked me, especially when the lyrics referred to a future in which our minds will be controlled by a daily pill and our bodies will go limp, as machines do the work for them. I was young enough to take the song at its word, and the otherwise benign orange label became part of the dreadful message. When I chanced to hear the song again on the radio, that label appeared in my mind, spinning nearly to a blur, reeling me toward a bleak and soulless future.

A song on a 45 typically lasted only two or three minutes, so, as I listened, there was often little better to do than sit and watch the thing revolve, the music insinuating itself into my imagination along with the sight of the label: Atlantic Records' worldly, no-nonsense graphic that balanced black and deep-red halves; the gaudy, exultant silver label of Bell—home of silliness, of Dawn and the Partridge Family—with its black letters and bell-shaped logo; A&M, ABC, MGM, RCA; Chrysalis; Elektra's butterfly in flight; Epic, Colossus, Mercury; the Capitol Beatles singles' interlocking orange and yellow swirls that oscillated, spinning me into an agreeable dizziness; the late Beatles' halved apple; Stax, Volt, Arista, Liberty; Reprise's steamboat, flags flying, smoke curling from twin smokestacks like fiddlehead ferns; Big Tree, Buddha, Lifesong, Dark Horse; Bearsville, Sussex, London, Motown; Gordy, Laurie, Lionel, Eric; Scepter, Charisma, Perception, Vertigo, Fantasy, Jet, Rocket, Planet, Bang.

Buying a 45 meant being able to hear, anytime I wanted to, a favorite song, and there was a hint of wizardry in a cherished tune becoming suddenly not what I heard now and then on the radio but what I owned, what I could hold in my hand and look at, the music mutely, faithfully waiting in the narrow grooves. But buying an LP was an experience of a different order entirely. It meant a journey: a pilgrimage through a vast landscape of music that was new to me. As I first lowered the needle to the vinyl, who knew what enchantments and raptures, what difficulties and disappointments, might lie ahead? An album could—and often did—turn out to be nothing special, an excursion to nowhere, a collection of songs that evoked little feeling in me, in which case I traded it to a friend, passed it on to a sibling, sold it to the used-record store, or simply ignored it, letting my eye, as I perused my collection for something to play, land briefly upon it, then pass on. But there was always a chance that an album would change me forever, or coax something crucial within me out of the shadow and into the light; it would harbor a power that, listen after listen, renewed itself and renewed me.

By the time I was buying records, this idea of the album as a coherent, unified collection of songs, an arrangement of ten or twelve tracks on two sides of vinyl that adds up to more than the sum of its parts, was relatively new—and, in recent decades, as listeners have been prone to download or stream individual songs, the centrality of the album as a musical statement has diminished. When I was coming of age, though, the album was it: to convey to a stranger the intricate dark webwork of your deep interior, you could do worse than name your three or four favorite LPs.

Because the many songs on an album were deliberately chosen and arranged for effect, any one track wasn't merely a single, self-contained tune; it was part of a larger whole, like one chapter in a book or one section of a painting. Listening to an LP, I didn't hear the first song as only a song; I experienced it as the *first song*, as an introduction to what followed—a promise, or threat, of what was to come. The final track was not just a song but the *last song*, a conclusion to a journey, an implicit comment on where the album had taken me.

The B-sides of 45s had their charm. Since I bought a single for its A-side—for the hit—it might take an exceedingly long time before I turned the record over, in which case I might find something hardly worth hearing, since the B-side was often a dumping ground for the pointlessly eccentric, experimental, half-finished, or dull—weak songs that otherwise would have no home. Occasionally, though, I discovered treasure. I recall the surprise of turning "Let It Be" over and encountering John and Paul's goofy burlesque "You Know My Name (Look Up the Number)." Flipping the single of the Five Man Electrical Band's "Signs," I heard "Hello Melinda Goodbye," a song that immediately went into heavy rotation in my bedroom listening.

One problem with singles was that each side could hold only so much music. The mastering engineer managed to squeeze all seven minutes of "Hey Jude" onto one side of a 45, but, three years later, no groove was narrow enough to handle the more than eight minutes of "American Pie." When I bought the single of that song, I discovered that United Artists had split the tune in two, putting one half on each side of the record. On the radio, "American Pie" was an epic narrative continually recharging and reinventing itself; in my bedroom, it became a two-act play with an intermission.

With albums, there were no such restrictions; the B-side was as important as the A-side. When I turned the record over, I might hear a continuation of the energy and themes I had encountered on the first side or find a compelling shift of sound, such as on Neil Young's *Rust Never Sleeps*, the first side of which is acoustic, the second electric.

There was often a best song—or a favorite, anyway. It might be the second track on side two, in which case my listening of the half-dozen tracks before it involved my anticipating, if only at the periphery of my consciousness, this better moment to come; when the best song was over, my hearing of what followed had a tinge of the anticlimactic, an understanding that the most exhilarating moment the record had to offer had passed. My feeling about any song, as it played, was informed by whatever preceded and followed it: "That was great; I just have to find something to like in this one before the pure pleasure returns"; "Glad that's done—now something wonderful is coming"; "This slow fade is almost over—then I'll get to hear that heart-wounding minor chord that begins the next song."

As I listened, listened, and listened again to an album, my response to the various songs altered; my fervor for one might cool slightly, and my feelings for another—maybe a song I had first experienced impatiently, with little enjoyment and much exertion of effort—could suddenly blossom into surprised delight. As social scientist Paul Willis has noted, LPs are designed for an audience prepared to listen "with a certain extension of trust so that unknown material can be appreciated and evaluated." Listening over and over again to an album gave its subtle, hidden pleasures a chance to surface.

Sometimes the worst song remained the worst song. There was something to be said for that. What did I expect, perfection? How could anyone ask that much? Sitting through the weakest song on an album, the flat-footed, earthbound one, I felt my appreciation for the strength of the other tracks confirmed and fortified. The least best song was clearly made by imperfect humans; if those same humans created the best song—the one that flickered with a divine flame, the one that would pull me out of my body—how much gratitude for such luck could be enough?

Let me therefore give thanks for "Butcher's Tale (Western Front 1914)" on *Odessey and Oracle*, for "Saturday Nite Is Dead" on *Squeezing Out Sparks*, for "Concrete and Barbed Wire" on *Car Wheels on a Gravel Road*, songs that, like the intentional, small mistake in a Persian rug, remind me that only God is without flaw—and remind me, too, that it is we faulty humans who make great art.

13 | *Expectation and Surprise*

In a poem, Billy Collins remarks on the unlikelihood of us encountering in songs sentiments such as these: "I am so beautiful / and you are a fool to be in love with me"; "You are so beautiful, too bad you are a fool"; and "you are a fool to consider me beautiful." Collins notes that—no matter whether the above thoughts have floated through people's minds—of the possible combustible mixtures of love, beauty, and foolishness, this is the one a singer is most apt to declare: "You are so beautiful and I am a fool / to be in love with you."

That particular dilemma is, indeed, a subject familiar in popular music, as in life. We recognize, from song after song, the situation of the smitten singer aching from unrequited love, at the mercy of his passion for his *cherie amour, distant as the milky way,* for the girl whose indifference to him makes him cry out, *Cupid, draw back your bow.* Journeying with the singer through such a song can be comforting because we are traveling through territory we know well. We are hearing again the old, continuing tale, albeit—if we are fortunate—from at least a slightly fresh angle. We come to music with suppositions; our brains are trained to *expect.* The ways in which a song either satisfies or thwarts those expectations are, in large part, what bring us pleasure. Moment to moment within a piece of music, as the lyric extends an idea, as a melody repeats itself, as a refrain returns, as a rhythm, locked into a groove, continues, as a guitar or piano lick arrives just when expected, we are gratified by the familiar—by something we anticipate that, in its arriving, rewards that anticipation. The repetitions and continuations create order and coherence, an implication that we are listening not merely to random noises but to a shaped expression of a human experience. The repetitions create centrifugal force: movement around and toward a song's center, toward the fixed point that defines it. Whole tunes, too, trafficking in the conventions of a particular genre of song, appeal to us by expressing feelings familiar to us from similar songs.

It is rare that a popular song veers sharply from the general direction it initially, implicitly, promises to travel—rare that it does not follow some path long since paved in our brains. Dylan is an exception; in fact, the kind of startled attention his landmark recordings of 1965 and 1966 received was due, in large part, to his disinclination to be predictable. Even if, musically, they were simple, relying on a few chords and conventional folk and blues structures, individual songs nonetheless veered off in unexpected lyrical directions, and the subjects he wrote about—a befuddled Mr. Jones, presidents stripped naked, Shakespeare speaking to a French girl in the alley—did not fit easily into any category of song that tended to hit the charts.

Because it refuses easy categorization, a song such as "Visions of Johanna" stays forever young; it hints at a narrative but operates as collage, and the gaps between its parts are spaces through which energy flows and expands. The song coheres because of the recurring refrain concerning the mysterious, haunting Johanna and because of Dylan's attitude—all submission to his imagination's authority. But questions abound: who are these people he sings of—Johanna, Louise, Louise's lover, the ladies in the empty lot, the "all-night girls," the night watchman, "little boy lost," the countess, the peddler, and the fiddler, not to mention the narrator himself—and who are they to one another? The song's characters, images, and scenes float in a shared musical space but remain isolated from one another, like the planes of a Cubist painting. The song allows us to walk around something and through something without our being able to say exactly what that something is.

Popular songs before Dylan—and, I would wager, most popular songs after him—can be filed in a drawer of our mind that contains many others of their kind. One drawer holds *got the world on a string, got you under my skin, got sunshine on a cloudy day* rapturous songs of love; another holds *can't help lovin' that man, if she is playing him for a fool he's the last one to know* songs of bad-yet-irresistible lovers; another holds *stormy weather, stardust of yesterday, crazy for thinking that my love could hold you* songs of gone-but-not forgotten love; another holds *someday my prince will come, someday he'll come along, someone to watch over me* songs of yearning for an idealized lover. All of those drawers are near one another in the brain. Other drawers, a little farther off, hold *that toddlin' town, city that never sleeps, dear ol' Swanee* celebrations of place; *don't fight the feeling, twistin' the night away, having the time of your life* happy dance tunes; and *over the rainbow* or *up on the roof* or *under the boardwalk* songs of escape.

We take comfort in a song meeting us in old familiar places; it soothes the mind. Still, a song's alertness to the musical and thematic imperatives it has set for itself— and its nimble inventiveness in finding ways of being loyal to them, even if that means straying from convention— makes for meaningful surprise. Such surprise is what keeps our minds alive, giving them new experiences for which they have no name.

"THIS YEAR"

The Mountain Goats

2005

The tune begins cheerily: a catchy ascending and descending piano riff, in a spritely tempo, that will carry the song throughout. Soon the other instruments—bass, drums, guitar—have joined in and are urging the song forward, a steady, relentless advance. Then the singer, John Darnielle, like generations of rock and rollers before him, is at the wheel, escaping, on the move as the day begins, taking on, as his own, the power beneath his car's hood:

> I broke free on a Saturday morning
> I put the pedal to the floor
> Headed north on Mills Avenue
> And listened to the engine roar

We've heard this kind of thing before. This might be Chuck Berry in his V-8 Ford chasing Maybellene over the hill. This might be someone born to be wild, born to run. But the singing intimates otherwise; it isn't full-throated and free, or growling or grounded, like the voice of Springsteen making mythology of trapped, anguished New Jersey youth; it isn't John Kay of Steppenwolf hitting the road with his "darlin'" to "take the world in a love embrace." This voice instead is nasal, tight, vaguely panicky, like David Byrne but without the implicit winking, with the ironic distance from his subject removed; it is like the sound—if the voice weren't in tune—of some earnest fan singing along with the song when no one else is listening.

The singer refers ambiguously to his "broken house" behind him and to "good things ahead." We don't know what is wrong with his home, but it might not matter. We meet him when he is already liberated from it, when he is cheered by the "crashing and kicking" of the car's six cylinders. "A-ha!" he sings—a defiant, cathartic laugh that seems to surprise him, "listen to the engine whine." He is journeying toward "a girl named Cathy," who, as he says, "wants a little of my time." That understated, even insouciant line can be heard as being delivered with a nudge, a hint that romantic bliss is imminent but that the singer is too tactful or chary to celebrate it yet. It is Cathy to whom he is escaping. Is she his savior, his last chance, as Wendy is in Springsteen's song? Are we hearing yet another tale of exuberant romantic idealism, an anthem to youthful escape?

This could become that kind of tune in the chorus, a moment in so many songs of melodic release and gleeful abandon. The singer might gently take Cathy by the hand or persuade her to hop in his car and peel out with him to who knows where. Instead, Darnielle sings, as if through gritted teeth, "I am going to make it through this year / If it kills me," hitting the word "kills" hard, with breathless exasperation. Then he sings the lines again, the same way. This song is not about driving as long as it takes toward a perfect, nameless place where one can walk in the sun. It is about surviving, merely surviving, and the chorus' dark ouroboros of a joke—a first cousin to Hank Williams' "I'll never get out of this world alive"—allows that one way to survive is to die trying. To get through the year, this character won't be depending on love, romance, or the open road; he'll be depending on his will and wits. And wit.

As the narrative continues, we discover how constrict-ed, familiar, and unheroic is this character's life. He is a seventeen-year-old boy who gets drunk on scotch while playing video games, and Cathy is a comfort because she has troubles of her own; the two teenagers are "twin high maintenance machines." But the comfort is temporary. As the day ends, he does not continue north down the road. He is seventeen; he has to go home. He must circle back to where he started, and we learn at last what he has tem-porarily escaped from: a home controlled by an abusive stepfather. As the singer approaches the house, he knows what awaits him—he imagines the look on his stepfather's face and is "ready for the bad things to come," which have replaced the "good things ahead" that were on his mind when the day began. As he pulls into the driveway, the car that in the morning powered his escape is no longer a help to him. Instead, with "the motor screaming out, / Stuck in second gear," it seems to have absorbed the dark human energies of that house: stubborn violence, rage, and pain.

The song could now present in graphic detail the next moments in the scene, but instead it discreetly drops the curtain. We are told only that "the scene ends badly as you might imagine / In a cavalcade of anger and fear." The word "cavalcade"—with its suggestion that anger and fear have been formalized in this family and occur ceremonially—introduces a grim, weary humor. The singer seems disso-ciated, distanced from the specific facts of the brutality, and, indeed, his spirits are already elsewhere: at this mo-ment when we expect to hear again the bleakly determined words of the chorus, the song instead detours briefly into a happy imagined future: "There will be feasting and danc-ing / In Jerusalem next year." For solace, the song soars far beyond the particular narrow, clotted, time-bound world in which it has existed thus far; it borrows, as metaphor, the ancient and enduring promise of a liberated and united people unburdened of persecution. In this moment, vocals harmonize and lift the melody to a pitch—and to a possibility of pure joy—it hasn't reached before. The song, however, has not lost its nerve. It is not escaping into unearned optimism, for this particular Judaic vision of an ideal future is, after all, only a vision, only an ideal, the imagined end of a journey of thousands of years. This hint of the mythic complicates and deepens the tale. The singer, like each of us, is the hero of his own life, even if he is only a disaffected 1980s California kid, and even if the monster he must conquer sits at the breakfast table. He has a long way to go, and he'll have to make that journey in his stepfather's house, and in himself.

Darnielle, who wrote the song, has spoken of the trauma he experienced at the hands of his stepfather—but in the music it is he, at last, twenty years later, who has control, transforming chaos into order, ugliness into beauty. The writer Tobias Wolff, as an adolescent, endured life with a similarly violent stepfather. In the acknowledgments that precede his memoir *This Boy's Life*, Wolff writes, "My first stepfather used to say that what I didn't know would fill a book. Well, here it is." The proof of Wolff's survival is his book. The proof of Darnielle's is his song.

14 | Adolescent Listening —The Songs of Ourselves

When I was nineteen, I told myself I would be different. I would always listen to new music. I wouldn't become like the middle-aged people around me whose musical tastes had calcified decades earlier, people who cared more about Elvis Presley than Elvis Costello—people who, in fact, hadn't heard of Elvis Costello. It wasn't a difficult promise to make; I couldn't imagine being stuck in a musical past, since I'd never been tempted to. I had always easily, organically turned away from a favored musician when a more interesting one came along. I was continually putting away childish things. In 1979, I was a sophomore in college and had spent the previous three years discovering, and being exhilarated by, one new musical act after another: Costello, Graham Parker, Tom Petty and the Heartbreakers, the Damned, the Sex Pistols, the Clash. I was starting to investigate jazz, adding some mid-period Billie Holiday to my collection and, not knowing where else to start with bebop, picking up a bootleg live Charlie Parker LP.

I thought of myself as eclectic and broad-minded. But my record collection contained no funk, no disco, no country, no classical, no proto-rap, no reggae, no pre-rock pop, no show tunes, nothing from Latin America or Africa or the Caribbean—nothing of what came to be called "world music." I wasn't much interested, either, in blues-based British rock or progressive rock or glam: no Cream or Zeppelin or Yes or Bowie. No guitar gods: no Jeff Beck or Clapton or Hendrix. My tastes were suffocatingly narrow, although within the category of snarling yet melodic or acerbically satirical rock too aslant to have wide mainstream appeal, I was open to anything.

By my mid-twenties, already I was feeling the strain of maintaining even that limited kind of openness; I felt myself moving toward a future of living in the past. I was beginning to confirm the observation of Daniel J. Levitin, cognitive psychologist and neuroscientist, that "most people have formed their tastes by the age of eighteen or twenty." The musicians I cared about most were still the ones I had been devoted to when I was nineteen: Costello, Parker, Neil Young. My personal pantheon had not changed. I was still buying these people's albums but, no matter the records' charms, feeling fidgety as I listened, laboring to hear traces of the spirit that had taken hold of me when I had first heard these musicians' work. Costello continued to be my favorite because, when I was eighteen, I had had no question that he was; he had arrived in my life then as if from a far star, a spirit guide whose songs were sinewy, literate elucidations of my dimly lit, confused interior; they ennobled my lonely and vaguely shameful adolescent befuddlement and rage. I had never before encountered music that spoke so directly to me that it might as well have been speaking *from* me. As the years passed, no musician came along to take Costello's place in my heart, and I kept buying his records, peeling off the shrink-wrap as I sat in my parked car outside the record store, poring over the photos and liner notes, then driving home, walking through the front door and heading straight to the stereo to set the needle into the groove. But these purchases eventually became acts less of zeal than of curiosity, then less of curiosity than of habit. After decades during which, every one or two years, I added the newest Elvis record to my collection, listening to it sometimes with excitement, sometimes with flickers of interest, sometimes with relief ("It's actually pretty good"), eventually he released an album that I did not—could not—listen to all the way through. I one day remarked to a friend, "I guess I like Elvis. I must. After all, I own all these records." But it continued to be his earliest music, released decades before, when I was in high school and college, to which I felt a powerful and lasting attachment; loyalty to those records felt like loyalty to my own life.

I felt that way, too, about the Clash's *London Calling* and Neil Young's *Rust Never Sleeps* and the three Roche sisters' debut album, all of which I heard first when I was a college sophomore. As the years passed, though, much of my music buying began to take on a vaguely posthumous quality: I was listening to old favorites who were continuing to record albums, when we all might have been better off if it were still 1979.

Why 1979? Because I was nineteen that year. My brain and life were conspiring to make me care about music with a kind of passion I would never be able to replicate. Sociologists, psychologists, and neuroscientists all point to adolescence as the period when the brain, rapidly developing, is most vulnerable to the pleasures of music and when we forge permanent links between the songs we love and our sense of ourselves, of the identity we are discovering and acting upon. Not only was my mental wiring particularly free, in 1979, to be fiddled with, but that was the year I first lived completely on my own. In my small college town amid the eastern Washington wheat fields, I rented a ground-level apartment short on character and long on views of the building's front and rear parking lots. I loved it. Owning no car, I walked—with songs playing in my head—to classes and work and the grocery store and friends' apartments, and always I returned home to my own space and my own silence, a silence I filled as I desired, with whatever music was my current obsession. I was learning what it felt like to exist as myself, freely, within my own life, and my education had a soundtrack: songs I could never hear again without feeling that whatever they were was inextricable from what I was.

Research confirms what most of us know by experience: the music of our adolescence maintains a particular hold on us decades later. The songs we cared for then are the ones that can evoke in us the strongest sense of nostalgia—a longing, perhaps, not so much for those teenage years as for the original state of joy when one's rapidly developing brain first took that music in and felt its neurons dancing to it.

"Oh god," the poet Brenda Shaughnessy writes, "is there any music as good as what you heard / at fourteen?" Shaughnessy, in that poem, celebrates the songs of Duran Duran, Madonna, Dead or Alive, Yaz, and Erasure—music that, when it was popular in the 1980s, I either was unaware of or, hearing it once, tried afterward to avoid, since it left me cold. But I was in my twenties then, too old to hear what the fourteen-year-old Shaughnessy heard; my emotional weather still moved to the music I had heard a few years before.

For me, there is something about the music of seventh grade, or of a particular month in seventh grade, that disarms me and makes me wallow in nostalgia, blissfully, unironically. I might even narrow the time to a single week—let's say the last week of February 1973. I was thirteen. The radio was playing "Oh Babe, What Would You Say?" by Hurricane Smith, "Could It Be I'm Falling in Love" by the Spinners, "Don't Expect Me to Be Your Friend" by Lobo, and "Love Train" by the O'Jays. Five decades later, if I hear one of those songs, a sudden, unadulterated joy overwhelms me. The problems of the present fall away; the present itself falls away. My imagination might flash on scenes of seventh grade, but the music is not merely a conduit to memories of other things; I am remembering—I am resurrecting—the original happiness of listening to the song with pleasure long ago. Why should those songs, from that time, have such power? Maybe they were popular when I had become old enough to listen to music with a kind of conscious attention that brought meaningful pleasure but when I was young enough to be indiscriminate in my listening. If something was on the radio, that was good enough for me: I listened. I had not yet been conditioned by experience to be skeptical of certain sounds; I had no built-in scorn. Also, in seventh grade I began to be interested in girls. My relationship with the world was altering fundamentally, and it is only by chance that Edward Bear's "Last Song" was a hit at the time and therefore was grafted for good onto the person I was becoming.

The popular music of my seventh grade year wasn't better than other music—by many objective reckonings, it was worse—but it was *mine*; it was in the air, and in my mind, as I was coming into full consciousness. It is impossible for me to untangle myself from it, or it from me. I am reminded again of the poet Mark Halliday; I feel about the popular music of 1973 as he, born in 1949, feels about the Capris' 1961 hit "There's a Moon Out Tonight." In a poem honoring that song, and honoring the baseball-loving, bicycle-riding, bumblingly desirous adolescent he was becoming when he heard it, Halliday recognizes that, even decades after the fact, "no amount of irony will ever quite ride the Capris out of town." Nor will any irony ever rid my town of Skylark's "Wildflower," a spring hit when I was in seventh grade. Whatever that record makes me feel, I cannot explain it wholly with references to the music itself. I would have to explain the intricacies of myself as well, which—not being an expert on the subject—I could never do.

15: *Adolescent Listening*
—Choosing Sides

As 1977 began, I was a junior in high school, and my favorite band was Supertramp. I was enamored of its sweeping, melodic, hook-filled, often richly orchestrated rock, driven by guitars and keyboards that were complemented by a variety of musical colors; the band even included a saxophone and clarinet player. I was drawn to the songs' themes of alienation, loneliness, and longing, especially in the work of one of the group's two songwriters, Roger Hodgson, who seemed sensitive, inward, and misunderstood, as I took myself to be. I also liked Steely Dan and 10cc and Electric Light Orchestra; apparently, I preferred my rock more polished than rough, more poppy than bluesy, with a hint, or more than a hint, of sardonic wit. I was still a little fond of Elton John.

In other words, my teenage tastes were, if not firmly in the mainstream, in some nearby ripple almost indistinguishable from it. I liked the hit song "Go Your Own Way" by Fleetwood Mac, and a huge marketing campaign was calling attention to the group's new album, *Rumours*, so I plunked down my eight dollars for it.

Then, suddenly, everything changed. My small group of friends began buying, and evangelizing for, records by musicians I wasn't hearing on the radio: Patti Smith, the Ramones, Blondie, Talking Heads, the Damned, the Clash, the Stranglers, the Sex Pistols. On the pop charts, disco was on the rise, but in my friends' hearts and, soon, in mine, this punk and new wave music—furious, inelegant, unruly, intimate and unchecked in subject matter and language, often darkly funny—is what mattered. The disco hits that most other people in school seemed to like felt pointless; they sounded impersonal and mechanized—repetitive music that dulled the intellect in order to rouse the body—and I wasn't much interested in their subject matter: shaking my booty, usually.

What a song was about mattered to me, since I was figuring out what I was about. I sought from music the news that, in my yearnings and confusion, I was not alone. I needed to feel that a song arrived out of an impulse or dilemma I recognized in myself. Sometimes it was enough that the impulse be merely to blaspheme or act ridiculous or petty when the world would have me do otherwise, so even the Ramones' cartoonishly brutish instruction to "beat on the brat with a baseball bat" felt personal in a way that KC and the Sunshine Band's pronouncement "I'm your boogie man, I'm your boogie man" never could. When it came to love songs, David Byrne asking, with giddy uncertainty, "Where is my common sense? / How did I get in a jam like this?" seemed more real to me than Rod Stewart instructing his lover, with casual self-regard, "Don't deny your man's desire. / You'd be a fool to stop this tide. / Spread your wings and let me come inside."

Compared to the disheveled spontaneity and ill-mannered candor of these new bands, the Eagles suddenly sounded slick and persnickety, Emerson, Lake, & Palmer turgid and humorless, and Boston calculated and businesslike.

I felt myself choosing sides. I was for punk, not disco. I was for the weird and marginal, not the bland and pandering. I was for what didn't make the charts, not what was on it. Such judgments gave me a sense that I was standing on solid ground, that I was a distinct person, separate from the crowd, with my own sensibility, defined in part by what it resisted. As a teenager who felt an urgency to decide what music he loved, and then advertise those choices through the T-shirts and buttons he wore, I was living through the process the sociomusicologist Simon Frith refers to when he observes that "our sense of identity and difference is established *in the processes of discrimination*. And this is as important for popular as for bourgeois cultural activity . . . ."

Yet if my judgments about current music set me apart from the great mass of people in my high school, people from whom, for various other reasons, I already felt distant, those judgments fortified my standing within the small crowd I hung around with: the three or four or five classmates who were my closest friends and whose musical tastes therefore mattered to me. Daniel J. Levitin has noted that, coming of age, searching for who we are, we find others who mirror our developing identities, and we define ourselves in relation to them, in part through music: "Our group listens to this kind of music, those people listen to that kind of music." The more my record collection looked like those of my few close friends, the more I felt allied with them against the swarming Debbie Boone– and Bee Gees–listening multitude; we were a band of brothers and sisters, a small, obscure tribe bonded to one another by a secret, shared knowledge. My defining of the music I cared about was a result not only of my listening but of my desiring to belong. As I slid the latest album from the Stranglers across the counter toward the record store cashier, it would have been difficult to discern how much this was an act of curiosity about the music and how much a show of trust in my friends.

In other words—the familiar plight of adolescence—my nascent tastes were nourished by the approval of others. It was socially safe to appreciate Devo but risky to say out loud that the latest Barry Manilow single had an enchanting melody.

It felt a little disreputable to harbor continued fondness for bands—such as Genesis, Pink Floyd, and Yes—that we had liked without reservation two years earlier but that by 1977 had been redefined as bloated and pretentious.

During my final semester of high school, week after week after week the top-selling album in the country was the soundtrack to *Saturday Night Fever*. Its disco tracks dominated the singles charts. I had no interest in these songs but could not escape them: it was as if they were being continually lobbed toward me from across a battle-field by an enormous opposing army. It felt necessary—an essential act of self-protection and self-determination—to hunker down amid the barrage with the protection of one record: *This Year's Model*, Elvis Costello's newly released second album. As I was listening to it over and over again, it had been a year since I had bought *Rumours*, during which time that album had sold millions of copies, riding the top of the charts for months, four of its songs reaching the Top Ten singles list. The record was nothing if not radio-friendly, so much so that I had wearied of it, to the point of thinking of it with suspicion. Why was *Rumours* so immensely popular—was it the power of the music alone or of the music assisted by the label's big corporate market-ing muscle? Why were so many people in school—jocks and cheerleaders, for instance—whose lives felt alien from mine fond of that record? Why could I turn on AM radio and hear, within a half hour, a Fleetwood Mac song yet never hear one by Elvis Costello? *Rumours* had become the sound of mass culture, which I had begun consciously to define myself against, for if I didn't, it might erase me. Was there something rotten in that record's heart?

A month before *This Year's Model* was released, Costello came to town with his band, the Attractions, and played most of the album's frenzied songs. Before launching into

"Radio, Radio," a blistering screed against unadventurous radio programming, he introduced it with a goading call to arms, a test of his audience's allegiance:

> This is for all you radio fans. How many radio fans are there here tonight? How many people listen to the radio in the morning and they don't hear what they want to hear? How *many* of you? That's not very many of you. There's a lot of Fleetwood Mac fans here tonight, I suspect. Is that *true*? Is that *true*?

Costello was my leader; I was firmly in his camp; I was so grateful for the existence of his music that anything he said I took seriously. Whatever pleasure I had taken from *Rumours* was, I understood, insubstantial, fleeting, and untrustworthy—something I had grown beyond.

Records that were popular on the radio had become easy to dismiss as part of an oppressive, monolithic corporate force silencing music that was more authentic, raw, and thrilling. In 1979, Costello—absurdly and inexplicably, to my mind—lost the Grammy for Best New Artist to A Taste of Honey, purveyors of the disco hit "Boogie Oogie Oogie." There was a chasm in the culture, and I knew which side of it I was on.

The problem is that taking sides means closing your ears—or at least judging something before your ears have given it a chance. If a song arrives from the enemy camp, it is easy to hear its flaws; if it comes from an ally, a musician on your preapproved list, it is easy to grant it the benefit of the doubt and hear in it what you had hoped to. We approach music through a scrim of preconceptions. If a record is in heavy rotation on the most popular Top 40 station, we might assume that it must be worth listening to; or we assume that, appealing to the masses as it does, it is the product of cautious calculation and lacks genuine imagination and passion. We like outlaw country but not countrypolitan; straight-ahead jazz, not free jazz; Stax, not Motown; symphonic music, but only classical, thank you, not modern.

It can be difficult to hear the music through the noise of one's convictions—which are "more dangerous enemies of truth than lies," as Nietzsche reminds us. I was convinced that I didn't like disco. I was convinced that I liked Blondie. What could I do, then, when the band—whom two years earlier I had witnessed bashing out furious, rough-hewn punkish songs in concert—released a slick, synthesiz-er-heavy disco track, and it became a hit? I liked it—and, liking it, felt my mind opening a crack. I was convinced that ABBA's hit records were frothy, substanceless confections, not worth the listening. What could I do, then, when Elvis Costello explained that the quickly cascading piano riff in his caustic new song originated in his admiration of "Dancing Queen"? I began to see that the imagination that creates good music does so through the absence of boundaries and biases.

In his book about the music of 1971, David Hepworth observes that the tribal battles among listeners during that year involved what such battles typically do: "the struggle between the instinct and the intellect, between pop and rock," as well as a conflict I recognize from my own music listening of a few years later: the tension between "what we think we ought to like and what we actually do like." For Hepworth, those who choose sides in this way are neglecting "to recognize the fact that this is music and in music the right sound will ace the correct thought every single time."

Decades after the music wars of 1977 and 1978, hostilities have long since ceased, but the music remains. In

2020, Costello said of "Boogie Oogie Oogie," by the band that beat him for a Grammy forty-one years earlier, "That was a really good record! In fact, that was in some ways more punk to give it to them than it would have been to give it to me. . . . I think it was totally appropriate." As for me, I still like Fleetwood Mac's "Go Your Own Way," and I do not worry that my affection for it betrays a cause, least of all the cause of being true to myself. The record still has the right sounds: the jangly guitar, the cracking, tumbling drums, the cry in Lindsey Buckingham's voice in the verses that mounts to rage in the chorus. These sounds are not far removed from those of the records I liked in the late '70s that weren't hits—that I liked in part because they weren't hits.

I also admit now to being fond of the spare, strange guitar solo in the Commodores' "Easy." I like the soaring, swooping melodic ride and harmonies in the chorus of ABBA's "Knowing Me, Knowing You." And about the joyously busy horn charts and ecstatically unfettered vocals of the Emotions' "Best of My Love," number one in the summer of '77, don't get me started.

16 | *Songs in Time II*

In my freshman year of college, my Sociology 101 professor gave the class a challenge, an ungraded exam. He would play several recorded songs, and we—two hundred or so undergraduates in a large lecture hall—would write down our best guess about the year the recording was made and, if we knew it, the musician who made the record. The songs generally sounded old, really old; they had obviously been recorded long before I was born. I didn't recognize most of them.

I suspected that the other students were as stumped as I was. From hearing the music that was regularly piped into the dormitory cafeteria and blasted out of fraternity house windows, I presumed their knowledge of recorded music centered on Foreigner, Kansas, Boston, and Toto—recent bands distinguished by one-word names and portentous balderdash. On the exam, we all performed miserably. The next class session, the professor berated us. "You people should be embarrassed. When I was your age, I knew this. People should know this. How can you not *know* this?"

I could have told him: most of us hadn't spent our lives listening to Jelly Roll Morton, the Carter Family, Tommy Dorsey, and the Weavers. We'd been listening to the Beatles and Rolling Stones and whoever came after them; if he had played us tracks by the Monkees, Foghat, and Electric Light Orchestra, we'd have aced that test.

The professor's premise was that we shared a culture and thus should share certain historical cultural knowledge. That presumption—in many quarters—is now in shreds, questioned and impugned by academics and activists exploring and celebrating our cultural diversity and multiplicity. However, at the same time, the Internet has expanded our ability to learn about the products of any culture, including the recordings my professor considered canonical. The university students I teach, having no memory of the twentieth century, can nonetheless, within seconds, call up on their smartphone almost any piece of music, from anywhere in the world, recorded in that century. I wonder if people born into this new century—born into a world of instant access to information and into a society, perhaps, less blinkered and intolerant than the one their parents and grandparents were raised in—simply *know* more than I did when I was their age. I wonder how well my students, transported magically back in time, would answer my sociology professor's questions.

Unable to perform such wizardry, I recently tried the next best thing. Forty years after my professor sprang that exam on me, I did the same with a class of my students—although, I hoped, with less superciliousness. The course was a seminar for first-year undergraduates at Butler University, a class whose broad mission was to introduce these new college students to the study of the liberal arts. My sample size was smaller than the hundreds of people in my late-seventies sociology class; only seventeen students were enrolled in my seminar. Still, I hoped they had something to tell me.

I played them nine songs, each a popular recording from a different decade of the twentieth century, from the 1910s to the 1990s, and asked them to offer their best guess about the year the record was made and to identify if they'd heard the recording before, or were at least familiar with the song. I asked them to name, if they could, the recording artist or songwriter and to rate, on a scale of one to ten, their enjoyment of the song.

They surprised me—both by what they did know and by what they didn't. I was not startled that no one had ever heard Billy Murray and the Haydn Quartet's 1910 hit "By the Light of the Silvery Moon," nor that the class found the record the least likeable of those I played. (One student complained of its "old-timey" sound.) In fact, I had speculated that the degree to which the students recognized and liked a record would correspond roughly with how much older it was than they were; I also expected that the hit songs of the second half of the twentieth century, the decades of rock and roll and its varied relations, would be more familiar to them than those that preceded that era. I was wrong. What I did not account for was that, since all nine records were made before the students were born, they might all be essentially equivalent in the students' minds, all of them remnants of a history that preceded their own. What the students knew, or believed they knew, about the songs often seemed to come not from their having actually heard the music before but from their having kept at least half an ear to the story of the larger culture. They knew a collection of facts about twentieth-century music, and when they heard a recording, one of those facts, like a bird separating from its flock to swoop earthward, perched on that record and defined it for them.

For instance, I played Billie Holiday's 1937 version of "He's Funny That Way," and no one recognized her; instead, two people were certain it was the very different sounding Ella Fitzgerald. Could it be that they heard Fitzgerald's voice not because they recognized it but because some part of their mind knew that Fitzgerald was an important mid-century female jazz singer? Similarly—and more strangely—when I played Big Mama Thornton's 1952 recording of "Hound Dog," no one identified Thornton, but four students reported confidently that the singer was Elvis Presley. It is as if their knowledge of the fact that Presley had made his own hit version of the song overwhelmed any familiarity they might have had with his record, or his voice, and any ability to distinguish a woman's voice from a man's.

Nonetheless, those answers indicated at least some fleeting familiarity with mid–twentieth century popular music, as did the majority of the students' correct identification of the Beatles as the band responsible for "Strawberry Fields Forever." What most surprised me was that the hit songs I played from the 1970s, 1980s, and 1990s—the decades immediately preceding their birth—made them shrug and throw up their hands. No one recalled ever having heard 1974's "Help Me" by Joni Mitchell or 1987's "I Could Never Take the Place of Your Man" by Prince; in my memory and imagination, those singers bestrode certain years of those decades like colossi. The students rated high their enjoyment of the 1998 Lauryn Hill hit "Doo Wop (That Thing)," but none knew Hill as the singer.

Maybe little has changed in adolescents' experience of popular music of the past. When I was eighteen, given all day to think about it, I could not with confidence have claimed I had ever heard—or even heard of—Eileen Barton's 1950 number one hit "If I Knew You Were Comin' I'd've Baked a Cake" or Frankie Carle's "Rumors Are Flying" from 1946 or George Olsen's "The Last Round-Up" from 1933, with Joe Morrison as boy singer. Also, although I was familiar with him from the inescapable "White Christmas" and his series of annual Christmas TV specials, I am not certain I could have named Bing Crosby as the singer in the 1928 version of "Ol' Man River" recorded by Paul Whiteman and His Orchestra.

However, two of my students were able to do that—they recognized Crosby's as the voice on that record. Maybe I shouldn't think it mysterious that more people recognized Bing than recognized Joni Mitchell or Prince. Crosby, after all, not unlike the later Presley, was in his time an overwhelmingly popular singer and cultural force; quiet vibrations from the explosion of his fame might still linger.

But how to account for my students' knowledge of Frank Sinatra? True, Sinatra's fame rivaled Crosby's, but he died before anyone in my class was born. I played his relatively early—1947—version of "I've Got a Crush on You," and thirteen of my seventeen students knew it was him. More than that, the song was rated by the class as the most enjoyable of all those I played.

Admittedly, my survey sample was small, but I was struck by the students' familiarity with and fondness for Sinatra. Maybe, when it comes to knowing a singer, chronology is less important than the simple weight of ongoing cultural knowledge; no matter the year something was made, if it matters, it lasts. Perhaps that is the gift of our wired age: with everything on the Internet, and there to stay, it is difficult for important music to fade into the shadows. Are the music apps that are so popular with my students the means by which they learned of Sinatra, and learned to love him? Or, as a friend of mine theorizes about both the Beatles and Sinatra, should credit be given to the power of corporatization—of Sinatra being a brand, his image continually packaged and repackaged by major media companies? Or was the message of Sinatra passed along to my students in more old-fashioned ways: by some popular current vocal artist—Michael Bublé, maybe—sending them back to the master; or by their grandparents, as my students were growing up, playing Sinatra over and over; or by God sending the good news straight into their hearts?

17 | *Iconic Classic Boy Band for Old People*

The Beatles were a popular '80s band which my grandmother was very fond of, therefore causing me to listen to several songs.

— College student born in 1999

When I was eighteen, if I had been asked to express some thoughts about Al Jolson, what would I have said? He was probably the most popular American entertainer of the 1920s, three decades before I was born. I had heard of him. I might have seen a film clip of him, in blackface, singing "Mammy" or "Swanee"—or maybe I had seen only various comedians doing that while parodying him. But what did I *think* of Al Jolson? Nothing. I didn't think of him at all.

What about eighteen-year-olds born much later than I, at the turn of the twenty-first century? What might they think of musicians who were popular thirty years before they arrived on the planet? What might they think of the Beatles?

I was born in late 1959. Some of my earliest memories involve the fact of the Beatles existing: my older teenage sisters, in 1964 and 1965, listening to the early LPs and 45s on the family's portable record player; my older brother and younger sister and I gripping badminton rackets as though they were guitars and pretending we were John, Paul, and George; the three of us, on Saturday mornings, sprawling on the carpet in front of the television watching the adventures of cartoon versions of the waggish mop tops.

Later, when I was ten and eleven, just as the Beatles were breaking up, I began buying my own used copies of their records, catching up on the *White Album* and *Abbey Road*. As a young adult, I shared the sacred mystery of the group by presenting my little sisters with Beatles albums as Christmas gifts and taking them to see a theatrical re-release of *A Hard Day's Night*. When I had children of my own—two sons—I played them the Beatles, and, as toddlers, they got hooked, enough that my three-year-old, hearing a few introductory acoustic guitar notes wafting from the radio, could say offhandedly, "That's 'Norwegian Wood.' It's on *Rubber Soul*." I have never stopped listening to the Beatles. They are inescapable and necessary—in the air, like the breeze.

In 2018, during the term when I played those twentieth-century hit songs for one of my classes, I also surveyed more than 400 first-year students from across Butler University. I asked them, among other things, about the Beatles. I wondered whether these seventeen-, eighteen-, and nineteen-year-olds breathe the same air as I do or whether I might as well be questioning them about Al Jolson.

I requested that they respond to a simple prompt: to summarize, in one sentence, their primary feeling about, or opinion of, the group. About a third of the students answered that they had a fondness for the Beatles, and about half of these people said they loved the band: not a bad show of support for a group that had split up thirty years before these students were born. Another third either knew too little about the Beatles to have a strong opinion, had heard them but didn't care for their style of music, or actively disliked them. ("Overrated," many declared. One student, apparently intent on existing solely in the here and now, wrote, "Obviously they are famous, but not from my lifetime, so they are irrelevant.")

What struck me most was the great number of students who perceived of the Beatles essentially as *historical*. Far fewer people said they loved the band's music than expressed that they valued the band's place in history. They didn't think of the Beatles, first, as having made music worth listening to as much as they thought of them as having made a difference to the world. The band was "iconic," they said, repeatedly, and "revolutionary" and "classic," the kind of accurate yet generic labels that might be assigned to all kinds of things—the Empire State Building, Che Guevara, Coca-Cola—that are as important for their status in the culture as for some inherent qualities they possess. Several students cared most about the Beatles as being, in the words of one, "pioneers in the boy band craze." The group, I learned from another student, was most important for having paved the way for One Direction, a superior band. I had heard of One Direction—I think—although I knew nothing about the group; in this way, I was not so unlike these new college students who had little of substance to say about the Beatles. After all, in my almost four decades of teaching, while my students have brought to the classroom less and less awareness of the music of my youth, I have brought less and less awareness of the contemporary popular music that they care about. Usually, if a student alludes to a song released after 1981, I am forced to blink dumbly and mutter, "That's a little past my time."

It isn't difficult to guess why the Beatles, to many of those coming of age in the twenty-first century, might be respected from a distance more than actually listened to intently. Where, after all, would such people hear the band's music? On classic rock radio? Some Beatles tracks, certainly, show up frequently on such stations—mainly well-worn chestnuts such as "Come Together," "Hey Jude," and "A Day in the Life." But recent data show it isn't people in their teens and twenties tuning in to such stations; it's people in their forties, fifties, and sixties: people near enough to the original flame of the Beatles to recall its warmth with fondness—people like me. When teenagers hear the Beatles, it might be because a streaming service's algorithm has steered them in that direction, or maybe—as one student mentioned in the survey—their high school marching band is devoting a season to drum and bugle versions of Beatles hits. Or maybe they know the songs because their parents or grandparents are Beatles fans, in which case, as the survey answers indicated, their sentimental attachment to the music might mean a fondness for their family as much as a fondness for the songs.

Throughout my adult life, I have noticed that people born in the 1940s, 1950s, and even early 1960s understand the Beatles in the way I do. I don't have to explain myself. The Beatles are in their heads, too. But as one generation gives way to another, and then another, the cultural imagination changes, stowing in one of its far dark corners whatever once glowed brightly at its center. Al Jolson leaves the spotlight and, with his blackface and mannered, unsubtle singing, feels a little unseemly and inauthentic: a remnant of an era when people liked that kind of thing. In some not-so-distant future, the Beatles might be reduced merely to a symbol of a time that once was; they might be known solely for some fact we've memorized about them—such as their invention of the boy band—in the way Eli Whitney is remembered for his cotton gin.

18 | *Songs in Time III*

"The past is never dead," Faulkner wrote. "It's not even past." Songs are the proof; they are bottles in which the genie of a seemingly long-dead experience—its swirl of associations, its complex of perceptions and feelings—waits patiently to be released.

Over the years, I have grown up, grown older, but I have not grown past. I was eleven once; I am still eleven. I was seventeen; I am seventeen. I can look back at those ages and condescend to the boy I was, remark upon his naivete, his outlandishly unwise desires, his social inadequacy and ignorance disguised only fitfully by masks of impiety and irony. But then, after many years, I chance to hear Gilbert O'Sullivan's minor 1973 hit "Out of the Question"—its pitching and reeling, calliope-like sound—and abruptly I exist again in a moment five decades ago. I am walking through the downstairs laundry room of my childhood home, the window that opens to the backyard to my left, just above the washer and dryer, and the snug utility closet that fits beneath the staircase just ahead of me. The moment is an otherwise mundane one—why have I entered that room? why should it matter?—but "Out of the Question" is the song in my junior high head then, as it is now, and I feel again the flood of joy whenever that new song I loved was played on the radio; I feel again something else it had become the sound of: the tightening in my chest, the bewildered yearning for the brown-haired classmate with whom I believed I was in love.

Middle-age curiosity leads me to buy a CD of a Supertramp album that was important to me in 1976. When I hear the instrumentation drop away to only piano and faraway strings, and Roger Hodgson's strained and plaintive voice exclaims, "Mary, oh, tell me what I'm living for," I am not only driving my 2005 Honda to the campus where I teach; I am trudging again to high school in the dim, early morning, through light rain, drops of it gathering and dribbling down my forehead. I am singing the song to myself and feeling, like the singer, melodramatically perplexed and alone, floundering about for a private metaphysics to replace the Catholicism that has become of no help to me.

Marcel Proust knew about this, about the power of music to bring the past back to us, alive and vibrant. The example he returns to throughout *In Search of Lost Time* is the little five-note phrase composed by Vinteuil with which the vain, idealistic socialite Charles Swann becomes obsessed. From the first, Swann feels an intensely personal reaction to the phrase, as if it is deepening his sense of himself as a human:

> It had immediately proposed to him particular sensual pleasures which he had never imagined before hearing it, which he felt could be introduced to him by nothing else, and he had experienced for it something like an unfamiliar love. . . . [H]e was like a man into whose life a woman he has glimpsed for only a moment as she passed by has introduced the image of a new sort of beauty that increases the value of his own sensibility, without his even knowing if he will ever see this woman again whom he loves already and of whom he knows nothing, not even her name.

Significantly, Swann is described as responding to Vinteuil's music with the kind of reckless imaginative openness with which one falls abruptly and irrationally in love—as Swann does, soon, with Odette de Crécy. A year later, at a social gathering, Swann hears the piece again, played by a pianist. He learns at last the name of the piece and the identity of the composer, and he confesses to Odette that he has been in love with the little phrase; we might infer at this point that his passion for the music is becoming mixed in his imagination with his besotted feelings for Odette.

Much later, after his vexed and painful relationship with Odette has ended, and Swann is suffering in its aftermath, he suddenly, at a concert, recognizes the music he has loved:

> And before Swann had time to understand, and say to himself: "It's the little phrase from the sonata by Vinteuil; don't listen!" all his memories of the time when Odette was in love with him, which he had managed until now to keep out of sight in the deepest part of himself, deceived by this sudden beam of light from the time of love which they believed had returned, had awoken and flown swiftly back up to sing madly to him, with no pity for his present misfortune, the forgotten refrains of happiness.
>
> In place of the abstract expressions *the time when I was happy, the time when I was loved*, which he had often used before now without suffering too much, for his mind had enclosed within them only spurious extracts of the past that preserved nothing of it, he now recovered everything which had fixed forever the specific, volatile essence of that lost happiness; he saw everything again, the snowy curled petals of the chrysanthemum that she had tossed to him in his carriage, that he had held against his lips—the embossed address of the "Maison Dorée" on the letter in which he had read:

"My hand is shaking so badly as I write to you"—
the way her eyebrows had come together when she
said to him with a supplicating look: "It won't be
too long before you send word to me?"

Swann, in this moment, even while sitting among a
crowd of strangers, each of them listening to the identical
sounds, experiences the music as wholly personal, as the
means by which a private message has been delivered to
him in secret. By this point, the music is far less Vinteuil's
than Swann's. The lovely five-note phrase has come to carry the entire assemblage of feelings and memories Swann
associates with his early, blissful love. The music does not
merely remind him of a time that once was; it returns him
to the self he was then—since the past, so long as it affects
us, so long as it *is* us, so long as the merest melody can melt
the years, is never dead, is not even past.

19 | *Permanent Comforts*

Who reaches for a book when your heart shatters
into a million pieces? . . . You go and you listen to
Tommy James and the Shondells, and you disappear
into sound. Sound is incomprehensibly great. It is
the reward for being on this planet.

—John Darnielle

As our lives unfold, year by year, their changes impossible
to predict, we carry through them the records we love: solid, knowable things—comforts.

Thirty years ago, in the early years of my first marriage,
I lived in a small town amid the eastern North Carolina
tobacco fields. My wife, a painter, had been hired as a temporary artist-in-residence at the local community college;
I landed a two-year stint teaching high school English.
One day, in the town library, flipping through records in
the music section, I found a Frank Sinatra album. The only
songs of his I was familiar with were a handful of goofy or
swaggering or swing-for-the-fences hits: "Strangers in the
Night," "My Way," "New York, New York." For a long time,
I had known that I should give Sinatra a more serious, careful listen, so I took the album home. Fortunately, although
I had no idea of this, it was a record central to the Sinatra
canon: his 1955 collection of ballads *In the Wee Small Hours*.
Upon first listen, I became an acolyte. The warmth and elegant spareness of Nelson Riddle's arrangements, and the
intimacy and intelligence of Sinatra's singing—choice after choice of phrasing seeming exactly right, the sound
of someone feeling, in the moment, what the lyrics were

saying—were completely persuasive. I learned to trust that album as a place to go for authenticity, for a fine-tuning of my own emotional response to the world.

A dozen years later, my marriage ended. I lost my wife, but I kept my records—including, by this time, many by Sinatra, on vinyl, CD, and cassette. Newly single, and glumly so, having quit my job and closed my bank account, I spent the summer driving, a wad of cash in my pocket, a cashier's check representing the rest of my money tucked into my suitcase. I drove up the East Coast, across the country to southern California, and up the west coast to Seattle. Through all of my travels, I played Sinatra, blasting him as I sped past the smokestacks and rubber plants of Akron, as I cruised through the cornfields of Iowa, and as I descended into the alien orange rock scape of eastern Utah. My marriage had come to sudden ruin, and Sinatra himself had been dead a year. But his recordings had gone nowhere; his songs had not abandoned me. His voice was still there as my traveling companion and consolation. Over the next few years, through the nervous joy of new romantic possibility and the disillusioned gloom of romantic failure, Sinatra's songs—the ones I first came to cherish when my marriage was strong—were there to speak to me, and for me. "I never had the least notion / That I could fall with so much emotion," he sang. I believed him; I knew the feeling. "What lonely hours the evening shadows bring." Exactly. "I passed a shadowy lane / And I thought about you." Yep.

These songs, I knew, were contrivances, as any art is: written, arranged, rehearsed, recorded, and etched into lacquer, many of them before I was born. Sinatra himself, I understood, was a big, flawed personality. It may be that the best of him—the most vulnerable and emotionally perceptive part—was saved for the songs. Yet, however much his genuine sensitivity underlay his performance, the singing was just that: a performance, an act—as it had to be, if others were to feel something genuine when he sang. The trick, the artifice, did not matter. It does not matter. When I listen to the recordings of his that I most treasure, I take them personally, shamelessly so. Others have failed me. I have failed myself. But my Sinatra records—created in particular moments years ago but now alive outside of time—never have.

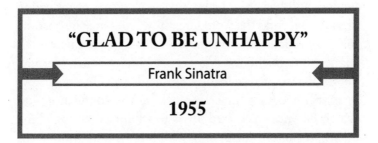

"GLAD TO BE UNHAPPY"

Frank Sinatra

1955

The delicate, bell-like sounds of a celesta begin the proceedings, accompanied by bass and piano. The feeling created by this Nelson Riddle arrangement is warm, enclosed, and intimate—and then becomes even more so as all but piano falls away, ceding attention to the singer. At Sinatra's first words, "Look at yourself . . . ," already we would not be blamed for sensing that he is addressing himself—as indeed he is; we are merely eavesdroppers. Both gladness and unhappiness are in the title of this Rodgers and Hart tune, and, from the start, singing with the familiar precision, inwardness, and understatement he brought to ballads, Sinatra conveys each of those competing emotions; they remain in delicate balance until the final note. "If you had a sense of humor," Sinatra mildly chastises himself, "you would laugh to beat the band." Although he claims to lack a sense of humor, the very making of the claim is an argument against itself. The accusation is drolly self-knowing; it's kind of funny—as is the reliance on the breezy idioms "look at yourself" and "to beat the band." This is not someone so unhappy that he cannot poke fun at his unhappiness. The instrumentation joins in the joshing: when the celesta answers each line of the introductory verse, it sounds like a teasing titter.

The singer asks himself rhetorically, "Do you still believe the rumor / That romance is simply grand?" Well, maybe he does still believe, a little. Sinatra elongates the vowel in "grand" and sings the word forcefully, like someone opening his arms wide to embrace the world; for at least a note—the highest one in the song so far—a hint of Ethel Merman enters the song. One implication: this disillusioned lover is still needling himself, mocking the confidence with which he once celebrated love's possibilities; he can think of his previous idealism only with bitterness. However, the way the melody rises to the held note of "grand" allows for another equally plausible possibility: that there is, in fact, something grand even about what the singer is experiencing now. Detach Sinatra's singing of "romance is simply grand" from the lines that surround it, and it sounds unironic and convincing. The singer may be disillusioned, but the ghost of his illusion—his happiness—lingers.

No song can be entirely maudlin that contains the word "toothpaste." In a pitying taunt, Sinatra sings, as if to his reflection, "You have lost that bright toothpaste grin." The image seems borrowed from an advertisement; it feels hyperbolic, false, even slightly ghastly. "Bright toothpaste grin" is an awkward trio of words, certainly a challenge to sing with any smoothness, since the four syllables do not align neatly with the beats, and since the phrase contains two unusual clusters of consonant sounds for the mouth to navigate: two *T*s side by side as the first word gives way to the second, and four separate consonant sounds in a row to enunciate as the second gives way to the third. There is a mildly grotesque humor here—and, interestingly, the joke is on the unthinkingly happy person the singer used to be. That kind of empty gladness is past; any gladness that can be trusted now can come only in the midst of the singer's unhappiness.

As the chorus begins, Lorenz Hart's words are wryly self-aware: "Fools rush in," Sinatra sings, borrowing, as many before have done, from Alexander Pope's line "For fools rush in where angels fear to tread." Here, the allusion is cause for a sudden, unabashed admission: "Fools rush in, so here I am / Very glad to be unhappy." Sinatra's voice quavers noticeably in the first three words, as if the force of his misery might overwhelm his ability to articulate it.

It is in a single line of the bridge that the song's conflicting emotions are, to my ear, most powerfully and delightfully expressed. "Unrequited love's a bore," Sinatra first claims, and then—seeming rather to like the idea—announces, "And I've got it pretty bad." The notes of this line descend steadily in small intervals; the melody, anyway, seems convinced of the thwarted lover's melancholy. However, while Sinatra's intonation admits to such sadness, it also contains a kind of wink, as if he's making fun of his moping, enjoying the drama of it.

As the lyric nears its end, the odd tone of tongue-in-cheek dejectedness continues. Risking mawkishness, the singer compares himself to a "straying baby lamb," but not just any such lamb—one "with no mammy and no pappy." It might occur to us that one does not typically think of lambs' parents as their mammies and pappies. There seems only one reason for the word "pappy" to appear here: to provide a rhyme for the upcoming "unhappy." But there is also perhaps a second reason: the rhyme feels so close to being laughably inept that there is some joy in our feeling that Hart just barely gets away with it. He might have felt that way, too.

As the song concludes, the words "unhappy" and "glad" return, and Rodgers and Hart cleverly make those feelings seem not competing opposites but necessary, inextricable complements to each other. At the word "unhappy," many other songwriters would bend the melody toward a low note. However, in this case, the melody rises to its highest pitch, and at the word "glad," it sinks to its lowest. The words say one thing, the melody another; the confusion of feelings is maintained until the end.

Until his final note, with the emotional intelligence of his singing, Sinatra does justice to the tensions present in the written song. He fulfills what Michael Feinstein describes as the obligation of a singer: to "engender empathy, not a standing ovation."

Part Three
The Song's Self

20 | *The Song As Riddle, The Self As Riddle*

Invisible, without palpable form, a song, unimpeded, enters our ear; then, if its sounds seduce us sufficiently, we open ourselves to the song completely: we are defenseless against it. Within us, it takes a shape that borrows from the shapes that exist there already, the peculiar contours of our feelings, memories, and imaginings.

Any sound, or combination of sounds, in a song—the crystalline timbre of the flute; the singer's kittenish lilt that shifts abruptly to a growl; the tension that builds, then breaks, as the chorus approaches and explodes—can lift into consciousness a part of ourselves that otherwise lies hidden, as the fine powder that detectives dust a surface with reveals the hidden fingerprint.

A song that haunts is not merely the pleasing vehicle for delivery of a message. Even a song with lyrics operates largely beyond words. It might contain ideas, but it is, itself, not an idea; it is an intense, compact rendering in sound of what it feels like to exist in a given moment or situation. Its pleasures may be partly intellectual, but they are first, and unavoidably, sensual—the pleasures the body knows—so whatever a song is about is something one's whole being, not just one's intellect, recognizes. The song is a complex experience, unparaphrasable and incompletely fathomable—and dynamic: it moves. Everything in it but the words—its rhythmic patterns, harmonies, melodic turns— is the sound of the song saying what words, alone, cannot. Thus, the song summons the parts of ourselves—shreds of memory, flutterings of feelings—that are equally obscure, shifting, and inscrutable, the parts of ourselves that language cannot name, that make us feel in the presence of the inexplicable. As songwriter Joe Henry says, a song is "not about *dispelling* mystery; it's about *abiding* mystery."

Music has the power to deliver us to the present, to an intense awareness of ourselves, in this passing moment, as breathing, feeling, complete beings. It returns us to a condition of wonder. It is this kind of undiluted *aliveness* that the nineteenth-century British writer Walter Pater held out as his ideal: "Not the fruit of experience, but experience itself, is the end. A counted number of pulses only is given to us of a variegated, dramatic life. . . . To burn always with this hard, gemlike flame, to maintain this ecstasy, is success in life."

It is no coincidence that Pater was deeply interested in music, which he celebrated as an art that intensifies our experience of the present—as the only art that successfully transcends the habits, structures, and limitations of the "mere intelligence." "All art," he famously claimed, "constantly aspires towards the condition of music."

To be alive to the moment, alive to one's whole self, means to feel the vertiginous effects of uncertainty and paradox, to be ensnared in a web of conflicting feelings. Since it communicates in multiple ways at once, a song can enact such tensions. Its harmonies, for instance, pleasingly unite different sounds, but each of those individual pitches—to do its work—continues nonetheless to exist in isolation, separate from the others; the beauty of harmony is the beauty of elements achieving a delicate and only tentative balance.

Songs that lack the tense equilibrium of contradictory impulses often quickly lose their charm for me. The willfully mythic or anthemic—any one of a number of songs by Bruce Springsteen or U2, for instance—I might admire from a distance, but it cannot incapacitate my defenses. It might bring me to my feet but never to my knees. Worse are showy, flamboyant songs, convinced of their magnificence, that topple from the weight of one-sided feelings. Queen's "We Are the Champions" and "We Will Rock You" are examples; their lyrics and music—both full of aggressive self-congratulation—say the same thing, so they collapse into themselves. One might argue that the source of such songs' energy is a kind of camp irony, but if that source is there, it feels too far removed from the sonic activity of the song itself to infuse it with the power of complex emotion.

Another way of saying it is that the songs that find their way most deeply into my consciousness and stay there contain a certain strain of humility, a recognition that the experiences they deal with are complex, contradictory ones beyond the musicians' complete control and understanding. Such songs, as Keats wrote, in reference to the greatest works of literature, are able to exist "in uncertainties, mysteries, doubts, without any irritable reaching after fact and reason." Often, the songs that root themselves most stubbornly in my psyche are ones whose pleasures are inextricable from some conflict within them, some paradox they cannot resolve, some riddle they are content not to answer and that appeals to me probably because it reminds me of the riddle I am to myself.

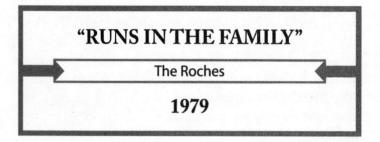

"RUNS IN THE FAMILY"

The Roches

1979

"I can't get over what I saw." These are the first words we hear, an utterance of intense subjectivity, anchored by those two singular, first-person pronouns. This is an "I" contemplating the "I," a self in the present moment feeling its inextricable link to the self of the past. Yet something tugs against this inwardness. From the first syllable, the lyric's emphasis on the sole self is contradicted—or, better, complicated—by the fact that the words are sung by three separate voices, three separate selves, joined in harmony.

The singers are sisters: Maggie, Suzzy, and Terre, holding the low, middle, and high parts, respectively. Their voices' complementary timbres alchemize into the kind of unforced and unreplicable beauty we expect from sibling singers, whether they be the brothers Everly, Wilson, Neville, or Gibb or the sisters Pointer or Andrews. These three voices belong together.

Paradoxically, the subject of "Runs in the Family" is the urge to go solo: the yearning that each family member, in turn, feels to escape the fold, to forsake the comfort of the group for the risks of "the danger zone." Throughout the song, as the words refer to this inescapable desire to journey away from others and toward the self, whatever that self might become, the harmonizing reminds us that, wherever we go, we carry our family with us. The instrumentation is spare: for the most part only an acoustic guitar, fingerpicked. (Late in the song, a triangle is struck lightly a couple of times for color.) The simplicity of this accompaniment allows the voices to predominate: each of the three is inescapably present, high in the mix; each has an equal and simultaneous say in this matter.

"I can't get over what I saw." What did she—what did *they*—see? They don't say, as if this "what" is too large to be contained in words, as if it might be all of reality itself, all that is available to be discovered if one looks in the right direction. It is, after all, something impossible to get over, as the wonderful second line confirms—wonderful in the way the line is witty yet sung full-throatedly, with earnest resolve and honest heartache: "I can't change the law of averages." The statement introduces a sense of determinism, of fatedness, which the next line—"I'm going down"— underscores; it descends from a high to a low note, and that falling feels at one with an unavoidable submission to something overwhelming. It is a force this daughter's uncle and father submitted to before her, a habit of restless exploration that she is beginning to fear "runs in the family."

The second verse continues to dramatize the tension between the singular and the plural, the individual child and the family of which she is a part. The first line, "One by one we left home," calls attention to each person—each "one"— in turn, yet the reference to "we" affirms the presence of the group; in seeking a life different from what the family provides, each of its members, paradoxically, is behaving just as someone in that family would be expected to. The particular experiences of anyone who strays from the group might be unique, but the compulsion to stray is a shared one.

In the song's bridge, the rhymes are predictable. The words "school" and "fool" have been paired so often in the products of popular culture as to offer no surprise, and they have, in fact, already been heard elsewhere on the album (*The Roches*) on which this song appears. Yet something is unsettling about the context in which the rhymes appear here: "All the boys / Could have gone to school. / All the girls / Were pretty enough to play the fool." The implication is that in this family, maybe this society, the means to conventional achievement for boys is getting a formal education—getting smart—and for girls is relying on their sexual wiles and playing dumb. The poignancy of this dispiriting observation is intensified by its being made by three women; when they refer to "the girls," they refer to themselves, to their own narrow path not chosen.

Ironically, the path they have chosen—the one they have followed away from the family—is the one worn well already by other family members before them, and it will be a path walked, too, by the next generation: the last verse announces the imminent arrival of a newborn child who is also fated to "run in the family."

From first word to last, "Runs in the Family" is charged with an energy that flows from a central contradiction: it is the lament of an individual tempted to stray, alone, into danger, yet it is simultaneously a confirmation of community. In the song's final seconds, as if enacting one last time this tangle of impulses, the three sisters sing, together, the word "family," and they extend its last vowel, the three voices separating, each going its own way, as if competing to see whose breath will hold out longest—to see who will go farthest "out there." One sister—Terre—wins, barely.

This seems just; it is her song, after all. Remarkably, she says it is the first song she ever wrote entirely by herself. She had been singing with her older sister, Maggie, for years, and the two of them had released a great and underappreciated album containing devastatingly piercing songs written almost wholly by Maggie. Maggie was the family songwriter. Maggie was the family genius. In "Runs in the Family," Terre sneaks off and finds a genius of her own.

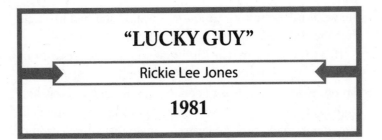

"LUCKY GUY"

Rickie Lee Jones

1981

"Oh, he's a lucky guy," Jones sings, half wearily, half wonderingly, as she begins her meditation on her cool, distant, unflustered lover. Then she sings the line again, her girlish voice curling tentatively around the syllables, as if she isn't savoring the thought so much as trying it on for size. She abruptly cuts off the diphthong—the rounded vowel—of "guy" instead of lingering over it, as another singer, as another lonely lover, might. Already there is a hint of friction between her and her subject, a disharmony confirmed by the devastating next line: "He doesn't worry about me when I'm gone."

We know now that this will not be a contented love song, nor will it be merely a sad and agonized one, although it will contain both of those emotions. It will be something larger than that, something extravagantly varied and searching in its feelings. This largeness of scope is present from the start in the rhetorical strategy of the language: instead of directly declaring her own experience and feelings, the singer insinuates them by depicting the very different experience of the lover who has left her, as if her response to the insufficiency of his love is not pity for herself but empathy for the man who has wounded her. She imagines herself in his place: he doesn't worry about her; he doesn't lie in the dark unable to shake her free from his thoughts; when he talks about her, he doesn't look as she does now, talking about him. If she were he, she wouldn't be taking things so hard. If she had his luck, she wouldn't be besotted and distraught.

These thoughts are the kind that could be expressed sarcastically and bitterly—there is, after all, a hint of Mark Antony–like, artful disingenuousness in her approach: *I come to praise my lover, not to bury him.* However, the delicate, tender melody and warm, intimate instrumentation of piano, bass, and drums feel completely in earnest, incapable of framing the singer's words as ironic or angry—and, anyway, she is not fixed on any such single attitude toward her loss. She seems instead, in the act of singing, to be discovering and testing what she feels. In the second verse, Jones abandons the project of imagining her lost lover's condition and instead remembers what she shared with him: the walks, the talks, the confidences. In only a few lines, the turbulent, dynamic nature of her pain becomes evident, as one feeling after another announces itself: insistence, as if she is stamping her foot in frustration; wistfulness, as she recalls the secrets that were theirs alone; a shaky agony; then an explosion of despair as she stops circling around the central problem and announces it loudly, double-tracked vocals thickening the sound as she harmonizes with herself: "I'm a lonely girl."

Then the song opens more widely. Instead of merely the absence of one distant lover, the problem seems to be bigger, more general. She sings not "I want *him*" but "I want *somebody* with me in the world." Then, after a short bridge, the song slips into an instrumental break, and Jones, as if given permission for a moment to forget the subject of her song, abandons herself to the music, sliding along with its movement and melody, seeming to be at ease in wordlessness: in her rhythmic scatting—*di-di-dih di-di-di-dih-dih*—and high, melodic sighs.

In the next verse, she sounds intent on collecting herself, regaining her composure, taking the long view: "I'm not gonna turn around. / I'm not his pretty clown." Jones admits that, in announcing her love to a man who she knew "didn't care," she did a "real, real stupid thing." The singing in these lines is anguished—she hits the crucial syllables hard: a *fool*ish thing, *stup*id thing, I *love* him, I *want* him, I *knew*, I *knew*. In this distressed delivery we hear her intense humiliation and regret but also a hint that she might yet distance herself from those feelings: Jones knows this old story in which she has found herself a character once again. She can predict what happens next: she will "cry awhile," and then she'll keep going. As if straining to grab hold of a platitude that might rescue her, she sings, "Tomorrow is a new day"; the belief feels almost completely *willed*—the tongue saying what the heart does not yet accept as true. Or maybe the statement is an act both of willfulness and of resignation. What else, after all, can this loser in love do but let time do its work?

Near the song's end, the singer surprises us: "lucky guy," she whispers. Did she just say, "*I'm* a lucky guy"? As if to erase any uncertainty, she repeats herself: "Hey, I'm a lucky guy." It sounds like a mistake. What has happened to the "lonely girl" she was a minute ago? How can this song of admittedly multiple and protean emotions have veered so far from where it began? We might wonder whether she calls herself lucky less to name a fact than to wish it were true.

Then a remarkable thing happens: Jones says it again, more emphatically this time—"Real, real lucky guy." Then she says it again, again, and again, each time differently, until the mere incanting of it, the shaping and reshaping of the syllables to fit the music, makes the words sound true, until they are no longer needed, melting into a serene, final extended "ooooh." The consolation the singer finds at last is in the music that, through her journey from one feeling to the next, has been accompanying her from the start.

21 | *Time in Songs*

Time is always new; cannot possibly be anything but
new. Heard as a succession of acoustical events, music
will soon become boring; heard as the manifestation
of time eventuating, it can never bore.
— Victor Zuckerkandl

Music makes us alive to time. One note, one beat, is followed by another, and another, and we attend to each
musical moment as it approaches, arrives, and vanishes;
in the midst of our listening, we anticipate, witness, and
remember, all at once. A moment might startle or delight
us, soothe or bore us, and in each case our reaction is a
consequence of what we have already heard or what we
expected to hear. Like our experience of the ongoingness
of life itself, but in compacted, concentrated form, our experience of the unfolding of music is one of expectation
and surprise, promise and fulfillment, tension and release.
Whether it seems to stop time, delay it, hurry it along,
chop it into bits, reverse it, or make it swirl, a song that
controls our attention enlivens our sense of existing in a
world of time.

The poet Ezra Pound wrote, "Rhythm is a form cut into
TIME, as a design is determined SPACE." This definition
applies not just to poetic rhythm but to musical rhythm,
which involves not merely a song's underlying meter, its
unvarying pattern of beats, but all of the small and large—
and pleasingly various—rhythmic gestures made by instruments and voices within that pattern. While we listen to a
compelling song, its carving of time into distinctive forms

stimulates our awareness: it makes us feel acutely the present moment, for it gives that moment a singular shape. As sociomusicologist Simon Frith writes, "[I]f 'the present' is actually defined by a quality of *attention*, then music does indeed expand the moment, by framing it. And it is precisely this 'time attention' which defines musical pleasure." Paradoxically, and necessarily, this framing of the moment makes us feel keenly the ceasing of that moment.

This tension—music's concern simultaneously with the present and with its passing—is central to why the songs I love charge me with emotion. They attend to wisps of feeling, fleeting ones, seizing them and holding them up to view. They make us slow down and pay attention. As a song moves through time, or time moves through it, even the smallest rhythmic disruption can contribute to our awareness that we exist within a distinct moment. Geoff Emerick, a sound engineer for some of the Beatles' greatest records, explained that the group often decided not to fix an error it heard in a rhythm track. "When everything is perfectly in time," he said, "the ear or mind tends to ignore it, much like a clock ticking in your bedroom—after a while you don't hear it."

In directing our attention to the present moment, songs make us feel how evanescent that present is, how impossible to grasp and hold. What is that thing, anyway, that we call the present moment? It is that—if it ever existed—which is passing now, or has already passed. Music, giving discernible form to our experience of this passing, implies a kind of devotion to it—time, after all, being the composer's raw material. This implies a devotion to the condition of existence itself, which is change, the cause of our joy and suffering.

Yet even as music moves forward, it casts its eyes backward. It repeats itself: a melodic phrase ends, then is played again; a chorus erupts, vanishes, then returns; one line of the lyric rhymes with another. A song continually travels to new ground, and its changes bring pleasure, but it also offers the satisfactions of recovery; it returns us to what we knew and briefly lost. I am charmed by this explanation, by psychoanalyst Heinz Kohut and musicologist and conductor Siegmund Levarie, for why such repetitions please us: "[W]hen hearing a phrase or a melody for the second time . . . the listener saves a part of the energy required for a first hearing. He recognizes it, that is, [it] requires less effort to master it than when it was new. The surplus energy is one of the sources which enable the listener to experience joy."

Yes: joy as a consequence of a song's pattern of disruptions and recurrences, not as a consequence of its joyful subject matter. This explains why I can take giddy delight in listening to an accomplished version of "Guess I'll Hang My Tears Out to Dry" yet am depressed when encountering the children's summer camp standard "If You're Happy and You Know It, Clap Your Hands."

"KILLING FLOOR"

Howlin' Wolf

1964

Hubert Sumlin is by himself, slashing rapidly at his electric guitar, circling for a landing, looking for a groove. Then other instruments—bass, drums, piano, acoustic guitar, horns—swoop in, and Sumlin finds his spot among them, settling into a fervent riff that will be the center of "Killing Floor": two quick notes, then a rest, then another cluster of notes, like something stinging then retreating, stinging then retreating again. Bolstered by two saxophones playing the same notes, that riff would hypnotize, it would be all I wished to listen to, if it weren't for the swarm of other sounds competing for attention. The bass and drums are unrelenting, filling every space, and Lafayette Leake, on piano, isn't just providing a central melody line—he is ringing changes on the tune continually, jazzing it up, taking chords apart and putting them together again, shifting his rhythmic approach with every bar. Each instrument is going at the song with full fury, attacking it—the bass and piano with agitations of eighth notes—but miraculously they don't get in each other's way. How could there be room here for anything else? Yet Howlin' Wolf muscles his way in, growling, with his voice of rotgut and ground glass, "I should-a *quit* you a long *time* ago." The manic sounds do not let up. The guitar riff is still propelling the song—nothing is going to stop it—and, underneath the first line of vocals, the piano leaps back in, loud and jabbering, as if reluctant to cede the stage to the singer. There is so much to listen to at every turn that I don't anticipate those turns approaching; I'm too busy hearing what is happening now—and now—and now—to be aware of time passing.

The Wolf sings two verses, grumbling to his lover that instead of sticking around and putting up with her, he should have obeyed his first thought and taken off for Mexico. He's on a roll, ready for a third verse, ready to keep ranting, and sings, "Ah—," maybe "I." It sounds like the beginning of an utterance he doesn't get to finish, for he abruptly surrenders to the band, letting the guitar and piano take over in a frenzy of thrashes, squeals, and plinks. Then the Wolf returns, completing his testimony about how his woman has put him on the killing floor, and finally, with a hint of contentment—as if relieved to have gotten all this off his chest—snarls, "Yeah." From the start, this song has been a glorious delirium, intent on outrunning time. And it nearly does. As the song fades out—already?—I begin almost to doubt that I heard it, or at least heard it completely. It was too much too soon, finished too quickly. I feel detached from time and unaccountably refreshed, as after those rare nights of sleep when I close my eyes in the dark then open them suddenly to blazing sunlight, eight hours having passed yet seeming like a second.

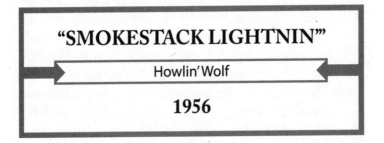

"SMOKESTACK LIGHTNIN'"

Howlin' Wolf

1956

"Smokestack Lightnin'" lurches and sways; measure by measure, I feel it taking its time, jouncing down the tracks, laboring to make its way across a boundless landscape, both physical and metaphysical.

Sumlin's guitar again begins the proceedings and is quickly joined by drums, bass, and piano. The instruments establish an oddly staggering rhythm caused by the fact that the main guitar riff starts on the first off-beat of each bar, while the drummer, at the same moment, plays a two-beat snare fill, complicating—even disrupting—the rhythm. From the start, the song has a vexed relationship with time, and it therefore makes me feel intensely the presence of time; the song moves forward, as it must, but seems hesitant to do so.

When the Wolf comes in, his voice—heavy though it is—floats above the arrangement, the rhythms of his sing-

ing sometimes aligning with the ongoing guitar riff, sometimes working against it, his wordless howls that follow
every verse lifting the song into something that transcends
the merely human. He becomes part animal then—a
wolf—and part keening train whistle. The song, after all,
at least at the start, is about a train. The initial thought in
the singer's mind, or the vision in his eye, is of sparks flying
from a locomotive's smokestack. We don't know from these
first lines that this song will be about sexual betrayal—and
therefore it already is about something larger than that. The
image feels archetypal, multiple and ambiguous in connotation; it involves a collision of the industrial (the smokestack)
and the natural (lightning), and maybe a collision of color, if
we imagine that it is a black smokestack emitting sparks that
shine "just like gold." Strangely, when the singer demands,
"Why don't you hear me cryin'?" it seems to be not a human but the sparks he is addressing, as if he is calling out to
some symbolic promise beyond his full understanding and
beyond his reach. It is also a promise beyond the capacity of
human language to express, for this is when the Wolf begins
to howl, the sounds loud and long, tortured and menacing,
slithering up and down in pitch. Is this a man or a wounded·
animal—or a reminder that they are the same thing? As if
in an ancient myth or fable, the singer seems on the edge of
his humanness, alone with the unknowable, the primordial,
even the mystical. The howls echo: the singer is in a vast
space, a voice in the wilderness.

He is also simultaneously in the busy human world of
love, sex, infidelity, despair, and indignation, for he is
suddenly addressing his "baby," imploring of her, "What's
the matter here?" And now it is she he addresses when he
asks, "Oh, don't you hear me cryin'?" This unexplained
leap from the initial image of the train to a focus on the
lover suggests a breadth of time and space; the song has

traveled a significant, indefinable distance to get from one scene to the other. Now, for three bars, the Wolf blows his harmonica, somehow unifying all that has come before; the sound draws attention to Sumlin's guitar riff by echoing its melody, and it has the feel of a sob or of the steady chugging of the train that seems, from the song's first notes, to have been approaching.

As the song continues, its two strands—the train and the lover who stayed last night in another's bed—are joined in the singer's mind. The train becomes a solution to his agony. He calls out to the engineer, either in reality or in his imagination, "Stop your train. / Let a poor boy ride." He might be deciding here to journey away, escaping his woman and his pain. But an odd thing occurs at this late point in the song: he says to his lover, "Fare you well. / Never see you no more," yet he goes nowhere. He stays put, at least psychologically, continuing to think about her betrayal to the point of demanding details. "Who been here, baby, / Since I been gone?" he asks, and then he provides—maybe through the help of his imagination—his own answer: "a little bitty boy / With a derby on."

The world of "Smokestack Lightnin'" feels so large that the song suggests it but cannot contain it: the physical landscape of seemingly endless distances from which, and to which, the train travels; the temporal landscape of the ancient mystery of human feelings and the myths by which we express them; and the psychic and emotional landscape that the singer traverses within himself, one of sadness, rage, impotence, pride, jealousy, obsessiveness, and the yearning to escape such things.

"Smokestack Lightnin'" is little more than three minutes long. My imagination finds that impossible to believe.

22 | *Time in Songs II*

John Cage's infamous composition *4'33"* contains nothing but 273 seconds of silence, or at least the silence of the instruments that the musicians are instructed, by the composer, not to play. When the piece is publicly performed, all the audience hears is whatever chance sound—whatever natural music of the surroundings—happens to occur between the beginning and ending of the piece. The only musical material Cage uses is time. He takes away everything but that, which leaves us the world and our awareness of it.

Why 273 seconds? Is this duration just a matter of chance, a phenomenon central to Cage's aesthetics? Or is the duration a conscious and judicious choice: just long enough to make listeners restless, and therefore attentive in unexpected and instructive ways, but not so long that they become merely weary?

Even in songs that contain actual sounds, the length of the tune contributes to the kind of attention it inspires. A song might go on for eight minutes or ten or twelve, padded by interminable guitar jams and organ solos, and the result can be tedium. Or the result can be giddy ecstasy—much depends on the song's ability to persuade us to follow where it goes, to abandon ourselves to its own sense of abandon. When a tune is noticeably short—which, in the context of most popular music, I would define as around two minutes, maybe even less—it might seem a mere trifle, worth no more than the time allotted to it. Or it might burst with pleasures and seem to be over too soon.

That feeling that a song has come to a premature end can be one of its chief glories. Keats reminds us that an unavoidable part of the experience of pleasure is a recognition that the feeling will not last: Joy's "hand is ever at his lips / Bidding adieu." When I first hear a song, and like it, and it ends before I expect it to, I think, *"Already? I want more."* The next time I hear the song, its pleasures become even more darkly rich because they are accompanied by my knowledge of their imminent end. There are songs so short and lovely that I ache when hearing even their first few bars because already I am sorry that they will end so soon.

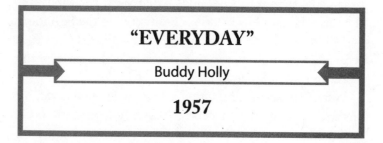

"EVERYDAY"

Buddy Holly

1957

There's something homespun and unstudied about the whole affair. A celesta—a compact keyboard that sounds like a glockenspiel—chimes brightly, riding the spirited rhythm established by stand-up bass and by Jerry Allison, who is usually behind the drum kit but who on this song merely slaps his knee. The presentation feels ingenuous, close to naive, as if Holly is a happy amateur who, suddenly in love, flush with hopeful expectation and the urge to sing about it, must rely on whatever few things are at hand to help him express his unabashed elation.

When the track was recorded in July 1957, Holly was only twenty, young enough, no doubt, still to recall the giddy thrill of adolescent desire, which may be why the lack of self-consciousness in "Everyday," its expression of guileless trust, does not seem put on. (The 1978 film *The Buddy Holly Story* is a patchwork of inaccuracies, but some of them are in service of getting the spirit of the music right. In an invented scene in which Buddy and his teenage bandmates are in the Holly family garage practicing "Everyday," Buddy asks one of them, the next time he's in the school's band room, to borrow a glockenspiel so they can put it on the recording. We are reminded of just how young and sheltered these musicians are: they live in their parents' homes; they go to school.)

The song might be light on emotional tension—it is all buoyant optimism—but it is not vapid or sentimental. Holly's singing ensures this. Cultural theorist Paul Willis gets it right when he observes that "Holly's distinctive style lay mainly in the restless, exclamatory, alert quality of his voice. There was no mournful submission to fate but an active confrontation with life and an awareness of the possibility of change . . . ." Yes: restless, exclamatory, alert. Holly first enters the song by announcing, "Every day, it's a-gettin' closer," that added syllable "a" giving the line a playful kick. Then, appropriate for a tune that captures a youthful, wild excitement and anticipation, he compares the love speeding his way not to a plane or train but to a roller coaster. "Love like yours will surely come my way," he sings, that "surely" emphasizing his unshakable confidence. A more conventional singer might extend that line's last vowel, in "way," over the final beats of the measure, but Holly—in his familiar hiccuping style—instead breaks the vowel into several syllables: "a-hey, a-hey-hey." His voice for a moment frolics amid the rhythm section, driving the song forward with ebullient energy.

After the bridge and third verse, the celesta takes over for a solo. The celesta player (either Holly's producer, Norman Petty, or Petty's wife, Vi—sources disagree about this), in keeping with the song's simple, childlike approach to its subject, plays only the main melody line, straight; there is no jazzy variation or syncopation, nothing remotely virtuosic. We might be listening to a talented toddler mastering the xylophone. The emotional and psychological world of this record is one of stability and domesticity, as if the singer is safe in a little room in which he can imagine anything and, with a kid-like, joyful noise, celebrate it. He asks the object of his adoration a question—"Do you ever long for / True love from me?"—but, before the question is even uttered, let alone answered, the song has already become a response to it, unfolding freely in the space of possibility, allowing no room for anything but bliss.

After the celesta solo, Holly merely repeats the bridge and first verse. Being unmitigatedly happy, the song has no need to complicate itself lyrically or to shift emotional ground; it stays in one place, a condition of innocent, gleeful expectation. Barely two minutes after the song has begun, it is done. Any longer and it might not be able to sustain its bubbly hopefulness; any longer and our trust in its joy might be shaken; any longer and I might not want to hear it again, immediately, which I usually do.

✦

A pleasure of some songs is that they are surprisingly, even extravagantly long but nevertheless don't bore (or at least don't bore me). Their length builds suspense or provides space for unexpected variations or seems delightfully, outlandishly bold, as when Van Morrison, in "Summertime in England," spends fifteen minutes working his way toward a destination that is nothing less than the silence that lies beyond our unanswerable questions. He chants, instructs, and cajoles; he tumbles along—buoyed by strings, organ, and horns that slash, swirl, and stretch out lazily—in a stream of allusions to Romantic poets, Jesus, Avalon, and

Mahalia Jackson; he shifts tempos; he slips into a spoken interlude; and he keeps time for a while by snapping his fingers. The whole thing would seem self-indulgent if it weren't such seductive fun.

"Hey Jude" is seven minutes long—at least twice the length of the typical pop single of its time—and, especially in the context of those other songs, it seems very long indeed. But not overly so. More than half of the recording is devoted to the "nah-nah-nah-na-na-na-nah" coda, and the song might have worked fine if that section were made to fade away two minutes before it does. However, the delight of listening to that second part of the song is born exactly of its extended length: the comfort—even elation—of circling back, again and again, to the beginning of the melodic line, and the accompanying suspense of anticipating Paul's numerous little variant vocal explosions, beginning with the pistonlike "Ju-Jud-ah-Jud-ah-Jud-ah-Jud-ah-Jud-ah-OWW! WA-OWW!"

Another long Beatles song, "I Want You (She's So Heavy)," ends, as "Hey Jude" does, with an ambitiously extended coda: an incessantly repeated circular guitar figure underlain by throbbing bass, crashing drums, and, rising slowly out of the mix, the whirling of a wind machine and a growing storm of white noise from a Moog synthesizer. However, while the coda of "Hey Jude" fades away, gradually and surely, the final section of "I Want You" ends abruptly; without any conventional rhythmic, melodic, or dynamic signals that the song is coming to a close, the music is suddenly, seemingly arbitrarily, gone, replaced by silence. A central experience for the listener is anticipation of this cold ending. If the coda weren't so long—a full three minutes—and that insistent final riff not repeated so often, the suspense would be less intense, and the number of beats one might guess will be the last one would be not so many. I am rarely correct in my thinking of when that abrupt end will come. Even after a half century of listening to that song, I—

✤

A song's length can have utilitarian value. Working as a disc jockey for my high school radio station, I was trained to make a station identification—"This is KNHC-FM, Seattle"—at exactly the top of the hour, to the second: eight o'clock, not eight o'clock and three seconds. Therefore, I learned to back-time: to play a record at the end of an hour that would be over in time for the station ID. That's why, two minutes before the hour, I often found myself playing the Beach Boys' "Darlin'" or the Beatles' "I Will" or the Boxtops' "The Letter." In extreme emergencies, I turned to Steely Dan's "Through with Buzz," a track I might never have played if it weren't a useful minute-and-a-half long.

In Indianapolis, where I live now, a local listener-supported station doesn't bother to back-time to station IDs. At the exact top of the hour, no matter what else is happening, an announcer simply interrupts the proceedings. That's why Astrud Gilberto, poker-facing her way through "The Girl from Ipanema," will suddenly find herself duetting with a clipped baritone: "When she passes, each one she passes goes, *WITT Zionsville-Indy* . . . ." The effect of the intrusion is to replace with the objective time of the clock whatever subjective sense of time the song has created. I like this station. I listen to it often. Still, whenever the top of the hour approaches, the quality of my listening is altered. *Uh-oh,* I think. *Is the announcer going to interrupt this song and break the spell?* My anticipation has broken the spell already.

In my car, as I near the parking garage at work, I estimate that I have about three minutes left before I will turn the ignition off, and, on the CD I'm listening to, I skip ahead to a good track that will end before I do so. Preparing to wash dishes, estimating that the chore will take about twelve minutes, I program the stereo to play three favorite songs whose durations total twelve minutes. While blow-drying my hair, I sing in my head John Hiatt's "She Loves the Jerk," having discovered that the singing and blow-drying will end simultaneously. I'm back-timing. I'm trying not to break the spell.

23 | *Tone and Trust*

I like Merle Haggard's song "Okie from Muskogee," recorded in 1969, sung in the voice of a reactionary, flag-waving, intolerant, fearful bigot. I don't like Merle Haggard's song "The Fightin' Side of Me," recorded in 1969, sung in the voice of a reactionary, flag-waving, intolerant, fearful bigot.

The difference is tone—not musical tone but verbal: the attitude of the singer toward what he sings. Such an attitude can be inviting or off-putting, nuanced or narrow; it can admit uncertainty and paradox or scorn them. It determines whether I will trust a song, will open myself to it and let it work upon me, will meet the force of its imagination with the force of my own.

One characteristic of tone is the degree of self-awareness or self-consciousness in the narrator or singer: the degree of distance between him and the words he is singing. If there is no such distance, the singer presents the lyrics with absolute sincerity and conviction, which can make for stirring results, as when Sam Cooke sings "A Change Is Gonna Come" or Percy Sledge sings "When a Man Loves a Woman." Depending on a song's lyrical content, it can also make for bombast or banality, from which a listener impulsively pulls away, almost defensively, as in the case—at least for me—of any number of performances by, say, Aerosmith or Journey.

"Okie from Muskogee," written at the height of the Vietnam conflict and of protests against U.S. involvement in it, pokes fun at hippies and draft dodgers, contrasting them with the good people of Middle America who hold true to traditional values. The song caricatures the young, rebellious people whom it presents as Muskogee's foil: they wear beads and sandals, have long shaggy hair, smoke pot, take LSD, burn draft cards, and partake in orgies. The details are reductive and external, as if borrowed from captions in *Time* magazine. The song's tone might be repellent except that Haggard seems aware that he is being simplistic, presenting a cartoon version of a complicated social and cultural rift. The people of Muskogee, too, as the song describes them, seem hardly real, as if they live in a Norman Rockwell painting or Li'l Abner comic: they drink white lightnin', "wave Old Glory," and, when it comes to loving, prefer "pitchin' woo." Also, if the singer who speaks for them is any indication, their logic is wobbly. Haggard claims that the people of Muskogee aren't hippies because they "like livin' right and bein' free," a reason that the longhairs in San Francisco might just as well present as an argument in defense of their own behavior.

The result of all this playfulness is that Haggard seems at a slight remove from what he is singing, and the song's tone is therefore appealingly ambiguous. What is his attitude toward the guy whose words he is spouting? Haggard might be kidding, and he might not. Each possibility feels equally true; the song makes room for both. The singer seems aware that he sounds narrow-minded, meaning his mind is wider than it might appear, and he even admits, before anyone else can make the charge against him, that he is a "square." If the song makes fun of hippies, it also makes fun of itself.

Haggard's "The Fightin' Side of Me" is different: it conveys a central, unwavering tone—an angry, self-satisfied certainty. Haggard leaves no room for the singer to question himself, even while his argument is simplistic enough to provoke listeners to do so. His complaint is against Americans who challenge certain unidentified social customs and protest U.S. involvement in war—maybe the very shaggy-haired San Franciscans whom "Okie from Muskogee" takes to task; the narrator of "The Fightin' Side of Me" might be a citizen of Muskogee who fails to get the joke.

The song is appalling. It is a tract that traffics in bromides and straw men, the most egregious of which is the familiar claim that anyone who questions the government's foreign policy is anti-American. The lyrics even include, without irony, the imperative "Love it or leave it," and the song is so general in its account of the behavior it finds objectionable that it could be complaining about any and all efforts to alter the American social system, including those to end poverty or racial segregation. All we know is that the singer is steamed about people "talking' bad / About the way we have to live" and "runnin' down the way of life / Our fightin' men have fought and died to keep." Haggard's tone is so convinced and belligerent that it allows me no purchase on the song; it seems inviting only to listeners who already agree with its small-minded sentiments.

Two Tom Waits songs, "The Day After Tomorrow" and "Hoist That Rag," also have war in mind. Both appear on Waits' album *Real Gone*, which was released in 2004, one year after the U.S.-led invasion of Iraq. Both songs are sung from the point of view of a combat soldier, and both make clear the loss and illogic—even insanity—of war. However, their tones are utterly different, and therefore only one of the two songs haunts me.

"The Day After Tomorrow" is a quiet ballad, its lyrics the contents of a letter a soldier is writing home. With its understated vocals and spare, tasteful guitar accompaniment, the song is lovely, and the ideas it expresses and the questions it poses are eminently reasonable. In one way, there is significant distance between Waits and the persona whose words he sings. Waits himself never went to war; the song's narrative situation and rhetorical approach are clearly literary conceits. However, in another way, Waits might be too close to his character, so close that his shadow risks erasing the soldier. The language sometimes feels so familiar in its encapsulating of the corruption, contradiction, and absurdity bred by war that the soldier might be writing not to his family but to his Congressional representative. He may be near the heart of darkness, but, in his thoughtful summarizing of his concerns, he remains, like the aloof, contemplative Marlow, at some distance from it, and he keeps us there with him. He complains, "They fill us full of lies," and he recognizes the humanity of the enemy forces, who don't "want to die any more than we do" and who "pray / To the same God that we do." These sentiments are admirable, but putting them in the soldier character's mouth feels like a shortcut; he sounds as much like a mouthpiece as like a real, complex human being. Throughout the song, the tone is restrained and sensible. I agree with every word; I only wish I felt them.

"Hoist That Rag" is all feeling, a febrile dispatch from an overloaded, agitated nervous system. In this song—with a medium tempo and angular rhythm, like a demented march—we are not at the edge of the heart of darkness. We are in it, commanded by the mad Kurtz himself. The soldier who narrates the song is not channeling the reasonable apprehensions of those who would question war's validity; he is channeling his own deranged and liberated primal self. Waits' singing is harsh and guttural, especially in the chorus' barked order, "Hoist that rag." In Muskogee, Merle Haggard's Okies might still "wave Old Glory" as an act of patriotism; here, the raising of the flag seems an act of desperate, psychotic aggression. If patriotism is involved, it is patriotism stripped of ornament, condensed to its essence of animal fear. Percussion fills the air with sporadic rifle fire, while Marc Ribot's distorted electric guitar drives the song along, following the melody but seeming percussive, too, its notes like the *rat-a-tat-tat* of a machine gun. Waits sings as if wholly absorbed into the character of his soldier narrator. In the midst of war's disturbed consciousness, and of his, he speaks in images that enact the horror of combat: with a mad holler, he proclaims himself a hammer God used to beat his drum; he sings of blood and flies and crying babies, cracked bells and ghost birds and smoke that blacks out the sun. None of this is moralizing; the character is beyond morals.

Waits' "The Day After Tomorrow" sounds true and right because it says exactly what most of us, in our own quiet, ruminative moments, have thought ourselves. "Hoist That Rag" doesn't give us time to think: it sucks us into the lunacy of war and, since it rocks and swings so strongly and strangely, seduces us with pleasures that make us complicit in that lunacy. Of the two, it is the most powerful anti-war song. If the smug patriot of Haggard's "The Fightin' Side of Me" were forced to listen to it ten times straight, he might begin picketing against the draft and volunteer to hand out leaflets for Eugene McCarthy.

24 | *When the Words Work*

The lyrics of "Elenore" by the sixties group the Turtles are good. Dumb but good. Good because they're dumb but know it. As the chorus hits—the arrangement swelling, the melody soaring, an angelic choir bursting forth joyfully behind him—Howard Kaylan proclaims the virtues of his beloved: "Elenore, gee I think you're swell, / And you really do me well. / You're my pride and joy, et cetera."

"Gee"? "Swell"? This is the lingo of a cartoon mid–twentieth century teenager, a real Jughead or Eddie Haskell, and "pride and joy" a cliché long past its sell-by date: the sign of an exhausted songwriter disengaged from his subject. But then that "et cetera" arrives, and all is forgiven; all is understood. It is the rare song that uses the term "et cetera"—that fact alone lends the lyric freshness—but, most importantly, its presence reveals the singer's awareness that he is relying on clichés, phrases so well-known and uniform in implication, a linguistic wallpaper, that he might as well abandon any pretense of effort and leave Elenore and us to imagine the innumerable other clichés that might complete his litany. The song is formulaic but not entirely so, since it subverts the very formula it employs by making fun of it.

Something similar happens in Ira Gershwin's lyric for "But Not for Me." The singer, moping about her unrequited love, would sound self-pitying if she didn't sound so self-aware. "Hi ho alas and also lackaday," she sings. The word "also" might seem a fumbling attempt to maintain the meter with a couple of empty syllables, but the syllables are, in fact, filled with wit; they communicate that the singer is not expressing despair so much as meticulously listing conventional exclamations of despair that one might find in the kind of song she is singing.

It is a breaking of the fourth wall, this admission by a song that it is not an act of spontaneous human expression but is, in fact, a song, and is therefore acting like one. Such lyrics disarm me; I am defenseless against the humor and surprise of them, so they enter my mind and stay there. The lyrics are intelligent, finally; that is what makes them persuasive. Intelligence, I suspect, is what makes any memorable lyric work for me—not merely cleverness (although that can have its charms) but a deep knowingness: a sense that behind the words is an alert human—someone sensitive to the ways the heart, mind, and imagination operate, and sensitive, too, to how songs work.

Puns can evoke groans, especially when the wordplay seems to exist merely for its own sake; we can feel simultaneously pleased and repelled. But the right pun—one that deepens our experience of a song's subject—can provoke a quiet delight. In John Scott Sherrill's "Wild and Blue," recorded most famously by the country artist John Anderson, the adjectives in the title apply to a woman who is yearning and lost and intent on feeling better, even if it means engaging in one rash, foolhardy act after another—even if it means cheating on the lover from whose point of view the song is sung. Addressing the woman directly, Sherrill writes in the chorus, "They could just take you up yonder. / You're already wild and blue." It's funny, this rearranging and recontextualizing of the words in the phrase "wild blue yonder," from the United States Air Force song. It's also poignant. The power of the lyric is not just in its inherent wit but in its suggestion that the cuckolded lover, whom we might picture throwing up his hands, is beginning to find in this frustrating predicament something darkly humorous. Turning a paean to military air power into a lament for a woman who is powerless to change herself, he conveys that his role in this story is to serve as sympathetic but bemused witness.

A similar reinventing of a well-known expression occurs in Maggie Roche's "Down the Dream," which offers us the comforting familiarity of an idiom and then surprises us by altering it: "There ought to be something to fall back on / Like a knife or a career." With the unexpected appearance of that knife, the worn-out locution "fall back on" is returned to duty as something literal, not metaphorical, and it intensifies our sense of the singer as desperate yet saved, in part, by her mordant drollery.

Music is abstract—it enters us directly, invisibly, creating a form of emotional weather detached from any reality but the music itself. Lyrics, though, bring the shared physical world into the song. They make us alive to that world and its implications and, in doing so, contribute to—and shape our understanding of—the feelings the music evokes in us. Sometimes, then, a well-chosen, precise concrete detail makes a lyric persuasive. I have never been to Liverpool, let alone seen Penny Lane, but the Beatles song puts me there—or in Paul McCartney's memories of it—with the specificity of the images of "blue suburban skies" and a nurse selling poppies and a fireman rushing inside to escape the rain. In "You Never Can Tell," Chuck Berry makes me believe in the reality of his young married couple when he mentions that they own not just any refrigerator but a Coolerator, and it is "crammed with TV dinners and ginger ale." In "A Soldier's Things," Tom Waits doesn't have to use the word "car" or "truck"—he implies the existence of a particular vehicle with his line "You can pound that dent out on the hood." In "King of the Road," Roger Miller convinces me of the existence of his hobo character when he identifies precisely his mode of transportation: "Third boxcar, midnight train, / Destination Bangor, Maine."

Such details persuade because they are acts of an imagination alert to the fact that the physical world is continually whispering to us, and the more precise the detail—the Coolerator, the dented hood, Bangor, Maine—the better we can make out what the world is saying. A lyric can also draw us suddenly, deeply, into a character's complex emotional experience with an inventive simile or metaphor, a comparison that explodes with implications that no paraphrase could capture. We feel the meanings fully only when the image itself is allowed to do its work on us, as when Joni Mitchell sings, "You are in my blood like holy wine," or Vic Chesnutt drawls, "I felt like a sick child / Dragged by a donkey / Through the myrtle."

Another kind of image merely sits radiantly in a song, generating power. It is possible to read such an image as a symbol or metaphor, but to experience it only that way is to dim its incandescent strangeness. It exists in the song because this is the place in the world where it belongs: "Raven feathers shiny and black, / A touch of blue glistening down her back" in Lucinda Williams' "Blue," for instance, and the "orphan with his gun / Crying like a fire in the sun" in Bob Dylan's "It's All Over Now, Baby Blue." Such an image reminds us that a song is not a secondhand experience, merely referring to a reality outside the song; the song itself is a reality. As René Magritte said in reference to the inexplicable collision of incongruous objects in his paintings, "People who look for symbolic meanings fail to grasp the inherent poetry and mystery of the image. . . . By asking, 'what does this mean?' they express a wish that everything is understandable. But if one does not reject the mystery, one has quite a different response. One asks other things."

The power of lyrics comes often from their compressed

nature: their ability to say much in a few syllables. A whole narrative situation and its central character can be conveyed in a few, brief strokes, as in the first verse of Aimee Mann's "Ghost World," which in a handful of phrases richly conveys the particular ennui of the smart, alienated adolescent:

Finals blew, I barely knew
My graduation speech.
With college out of reach
If I don't find a job it's down
To Dad and Myrtle Beach.

A lyric can say much in a few words also by doubling back on itself, using chiasmus to become its own mirror image. The effect is of an idea distilled to its incontestable essence. David Berman is adept at this strategy, as when he sings of a pair of ex-friends encountering each other by chance that they "stand the standard distance / Distant strangers stand apart" or when he observes, "If no one's fond of fucking me / Maybe no one's fucking fond of me."

In another kind of compression, a song's central subject isn't named at all; instead, it rises to our attention through hints and indirections, as in the standard "Blame It on My Youth," whose lyrics were composed by Edward Heyman. The singer, in despair over a failed affair, addresses the lover who has hurt him, yet over and over again he claims that the cause of his troubles was merely his own callowness. "Blame it on my youth," he insists, when he recalls expecting that a first kiss would lead to love, when he recalls that the woman meant the world to him, when he recalls that, unable to stop thinking of her, he forgot "to eat and sleep and pray." As the song continues, the experience of adoring this woman sounds more and more traumatic and overwhelming, until the singer's continuing contention that only his youth was to blame begins to sound like a desperate avoidance of the truth—or maybe a passive-aggressive attack on the erstwhile object of his affection. "Blame It on My Youth" never says directly that she was also, and perhaps mainly, to blame; in its refusal to say so, it says it powerfully and believably.

A similar admirable restraint is present in John Hiatt's "Tip of My Tongue," which recounts how a relationship was broken beyond repair because of a "slip of the tongue"—the singer impulsively saying "three angry words" that "killed" their love. What were those words? The lyric never reveals them. This makes psychological sense: the singer is addressing his former lover and is distraught, filled with regret for what he said. He is not about to repeat those words to her now. The fact that this is a song, and that we are its listeners and have a deep curiosity about exactly what he said to her, is not enough reason for Hiatt to allow his tongue to utter the words again. Their absence from the song makes us feel how unknowable is the particular intimacy between any two other people, and it makes the destructive force of those three words—whatever they were—feel all the more potent.

I like when a song, instead of telling me what to think, makes me think it.

No matter the splendors of innumerable songs by Paul Simon and Chrissie Hynde, two of my favorite songwriters, each has written lyrics that, in saying more than they need to, put distance between the song and me. In the Pretenders song "Show Me," Hynde sings to her baby daughter, "Show me the meaning of the word." It does not take long to infer what word she has in mind; it's the one the Beatles sang about in "The Word," as well as in most of their other songs. Since we have already surmised—and are thinking about—the word, some energy drains from the song when Hynde announces, at the end, "Oh, love / I want love." Instead of continuing to feel, with the singer, a hunger to know love, we become separate from her: we are an audience for whom she is resolving a riddle that we have long since resolved ourselves. The song therefore lacks the tense ambiguity of another Hynde lyric, "Kid," in which she asks, "Kid, what changed your mood?" and never answers the question, allowing the song to maintain until the end an ache to understand.

Paul Simon's "Train in the Distance" is an otherwise fine song similarly diminished by unnecessary explanation. The song's chorus tells us, "Everybody loves the sound of a train in the distance. / Everybody thinks it's true," and the image alone suffices to make us feel what it is like to believe in a dream, to long for that which we cannot have. But then comes a final verse, which begins, "What is the point of this story?" and the verse proceeds to answer the question, instructing us that the song is about the "thought that life could be better." In unnecessarily annotating itself, the lyric shifts from enacting a subject to explaining it; the song removes itself from the center of my imagination and settles on the surface of my intellect.

Another Simon song, "The Obvious Child," burrows into my imagination and stays there. Several times the lyric returns to a single odd image—"the cross is in the ballpark"—and lets the image do its work alone, without explanation. I appreciate how Simon, outside of the song itself, is on record as interpreting the image as being positive and comforting, while I find it unsettlingly menacing. I like how the song lets us look at the image together and leaves room for the possibility that it might be beyond the full understanding of either of us.

Don McLean's "American Pie" gives listeners a lot of decoding to do—almost every line of the song is an allusion. From the beginning, McLean has been content to let the song do the talking; he has not wanted to explain his meanings and therefore interfere with each listener's private relationship to it. In early 1972, when "American Pie" was the number one record in the country, I listened as a Seattle disc jockey, having tracked down McLean by phone, interviewed him on the air. The only thing I remember was the DJ continually, through various means, attempting to persuade the singer to reveal the allusions' meanings—as if the song were merely a riddle to solve—and McLean continually declining. He has been doing that ever since. In 2017, McLean was interviewed by Jim Axelrod of CBS News, who asked him pointedly about one line in particular:

> "But the quartet practicing in the park. That's not the Beatles?"
> "No."
> "Oh, Don, there's a lot of people who are gonna be heartbroken."
> "It *might* be."

Just as a mysterious, evocative image or allusion in a lyric can resonate with implications—with hints of things that might be—and thus invigorate the listener's imagination, the mere sound of the words, apart from their meaning, can carry a sense of the ineffable, of something slightly beyond our ability to paraphrase. This attention to the sound of words signals the presence of a sensitive intelligence, a mind aware of how language can trace, delicately, the feeling of experience and not merely announce the meaning of it. Long ago, Ira Gershwin recognized that formulaic, unoriginal rhymes can signal a songwriter's failure to engage meaningfully with his subject and his listener: "The words mustn't be precious or condescending. . . . A writer can't get away with the 'blue-you' sort of stuff anymore. . . . A good lyric should be rhymed conversation."

That is why, in a Gershwin song, we encounter endearingly inventive sonic repetitions such as the two-syllable rhyme in these lines:

> Though he may not be the *man some*
> Girls think of as *handsome* . . . .

Here, simple, familiar language is sharpened by Gershwin's keen ear for rhyme; the delicacy of the utterance's emotion is accentuated by its being given such noticeable formal shape. The subject—yearning for an idealized lover—might be one that songs have visited again and again, but the fresh verbal articulation of the experience can persuade us that this singer is going through it intensely, and for the first time.

Original, innovative rhymes make us pay attention to how the song itself pays attention. We might delight, first, in a rhyme's sheer ingenuity—that is no small thing—but, beyond that, in showing alertness to what an experience is truly like and expressing it in a memorable way, the lyric can make us feel again, starkly, something we had forgotten. The lyricists of the Great American Songbook provide innumerable examples—such as Eric Maschwitz, in "These Foolish Things (Remind Me of You)," rhyming "the next apartment" with "what my heart meant," or Johnny Mercer, in "Too Marvelous for Words," underscoring, with a rhyme, the singer's inability to convey the absolutely indescribable wondrousness of his beloved. All he can do is try, then fail, to come up with the adequate adjective, since such an adjective doesn't exist:

You're much too much and just too very, very
To ever be in Webster's dictionary

This couplet uses language to make us feel the insufficiency of language: the moment when the singer fails to conceive of the right word is made to rhyme with the name of the book that doesn't contain the right word, either.

Even the repetition of a vowel sound can do expressive work. Any songwriter is aware of the importance of vowels in making a lyric singable, but a deft repetition of such sounds can also invite the listener into the dramatic situation the song renders. In "I Get a Kick Out of You," Cole Porter writes, "Flying too high with some guy in the sky / Is my idea of nothing to do." The lines are built of an outlandishly extended sequence of long "I" sounds: six of them, each one aligned with a beat and therefore emphasized, with the last two—in "*my i*dea"—melding as the melody glides to a slightly higher note. The string of identical vowel sounds keeps the sentence in the air, as if it is the soaring plane itself.

An otherwise very different lyricist, Bob Dylan, listens to his vowels, too. In "Idiot Wind," he sings, "There's a lone soldier on the cross, / Smoke pourin' out of a boxcar door." With the multiple "o" sounds—both long and short—and the internal rhyme of "pour/door," the lines sound as if they are pouring forth urgently, sonically replicating the visual image.

Even if a song is dramatizing a literal, identifiable human situation, its most important work is to cause us to experience that which can be felt but not directly named. That, perhaps, is why we need songs in the first place. The most persuasive lyrics—the ones that matter to me—are those that are roused, not defeated, by the challenge of using words to make us feel what words could never say.

"SWORDFISHTROMBONE"

> **Tom Waits**

1983

The story in "Swordfishtrombone" can't be paraphrased because it is larger than the song itself. Maybe the story doesn't matter. The music hurtles relentlessly forward, as if on the trail of the tale's peripatetic protagonist, but it never quite catches up to him, or at least never catches up enough to make the events of his life cohere. The song instead is a churning effusion of glittering details, often flimsily connected, as if what matters isn't how one moment in a life is a consequence of those that precede it but how any moment in a life, in isolation, is uncanny enough to be worthy of attention. And if a life contains innumerable such moments, how can the distinctiveness of any life ever be communicated completely?

The song is the sketch of a character—a "doughboy" who, as the first line announces, "came home from the war with a party in his head." We are on relatively solid narrative ground here: we are presented with a character and a conflict—that "party" being, it seems, a metaphor for the unsettled mental state of a victim of shell shock. Waits sings the line softly, in a kind of half whisper, the restraint suggesting that what he is recounting isn't about him; he's just the reporter. But the music is meanwhile doing something eerie to the story—or to us. Bass, drums, and marimba combine to create a swinging, spooky, vaguely Latin groove that won't let up; the song charges forward, seeming to be continually on the verge of arriving somewhere, a place always just a step ahead. The sound of the marimba—hit by the mallets in a repeated series of four-note, then five-note, figures—is incantatory, as if the song were intent on hypnotizing us, melting our defenses, preparing us to believe anything. And how could one not believe this tale? The images are so specific and odd that the character feels intensely real. He owns not just a car, and not just a Cadillac, but "a modified Brougham Deville." He also owns—a metonymic stand-in for him, perhaps—a "mad dog" who won't "sit still." The man doesn't merely drink heavily; he drinks "half a pint of Ballantine's each day." Even when they seem unlikely, the details—because of their precision—persuade: Tenkiller Lake; Crutchfield; Oklahoma; Benzedrine; Lucky Tiger pomade. The vivid actuality of these particular places and things brooks no suspicion that this is merely a fable, some generic tale, we're in.

Whether the story is actually going anywhere— whether this loose collection of plot points will add up to anything—is a question the song doesn't give us time to consider. The groove that began the tune continues: it is pleasant and simple but obsessive, all about rhythm and percussion. Nothing is strummed here; everything is plucked, tapped, or pounded, urging the song onward to the next thing, then the next. This is the sound of incompleteness, of the impossibility of resolution, maybe mirroring the fictive character's strained mental state or even the manic inventiveness of the story's teller, who is starting to seem as important as the character about whom he sings. As if dealing cards swiftly from a deck, the singer sends slivers of story our way, one after another, so rapidly that we can't be bored but also can't be sure we're getting all the information we need to make sense of this tale.

Some details are lost on me. What is "a pair of legs that opened up like butterfly wings"? What exactly is a "swordfishtrombone"? Still, these words speed by so quickly, and have such imaginative, sometimes surrealistic power, that it hardly matters. Meanwhile, there is the delight the singer is taking—and sharing with us—in the wit of the rhymes ("He got twenty years for lovin' her / From some Oklahoma governor"); of the impressionistic locutions ("Chesterfielded moonbeams in a song"); and of the off-kilter allusions ("flyswatter banjo on his knee"). As the evocative details pile up, the song becomes not so much about the tale as about the teller: about his limitless capacity for invention. It is that story—of someone with a boundless imagination and linguistic gift—that we find ourselves pleasantly in the midst of. The singer himself seems to admit as much, as the song nears its end. He refers, punnily, to the possibility that only while he tells his tale does his character exist: "Perhaps this yarn is the only thing / That holds this man together."

That "perhaps" is important. This song is interested not in answers but in ambiguity, so it allows for the possibility that the returned soldier does, in fact, exist outside of the song. After all, "Some say they saw him down in Birmingham, / Sleeping in a boxcar going by."

But a final comment draws our attention again not to the character but to the fact of his existing in a narrative almost too fantastical to be true: "And if you think that you can tell a bigger tale," Waits sings, "I swear to God you'd have to tell a lie." With his last words, the singer emphasizes not the meaning, moral, or purpose of his story, nothing so reductive and earthbound as that, but the strangeness—the "big"-ness—of it, and the very telling of it. This claim is followed by a wordless, scratchy yowl, as if at last the song has become completely about the singer, about his own immersion in the story he's been telling and the music that has been hurtling him through it. After this, the record does not end, exactly—the sound fades, further underscoring the song's sense of incompleteness and irresolution, of journeying somewhere it will never get to. Our attention turns elsewhere, but the story might yet be continuing without us, at least while the teller's will and imagination hold out; this is the kind of tale he could unfold indefinitely, for as long as his character's life—or his own—lasts.

25 | *Fade Away*

A record is a fiction, a fabricated space in which, if we are lucky, we imagine the presence of genuine feeling. It is an arrangement of musical gestures, the sounds of instruments and human voices, but also of studio tricks: splices, overdubs, loops, samples, echoes—any number of sounds gathered and mixed to make us feel we are hearing a single, organically unified expressive act. One common strategy that brings attention to the manipulated, unnatural quality of records is to end a song with a slow, steady diminution of volume: a fade-out. This can be useful for disc jockeys, making it easy for them to mix the end of one song with the beginning of another; the fade-out allows radio DJs to talk over a record's last few measures or even to fade the song early themselves, just in time for the news or the next commercial or the station identification, but for people listening to a record on their own, the fade-out can seem to be no ending at all: an anticlimax, a failure of invention, a decision not to make a decision about where the song has been leading all along.

In one of his early Capitol recordings, from 1953, Frank Sinatra seems, winkingly, to convey this kind of disappointment. Near the end of the song "Ya Better Stop!", as the fade begins, he drops out of character and exclaims, "Oh, here now! This is not gonna be another one of those fadeaway records! Get your grimy hand off that dial, man!"

Sinatra admits out loud what we are not always fully conscious of as we listen to a record: that we are listening to a record. Pulled into the hallucinatory space that a song creates, we have good reason not to break the spell by visualizing the singer's lips near the microphone, the baffles around the drum kit, or the engineer's fingers on the fader bar.

The fade-out, though, does not always feel like an easy, heedless habit; sometimes it feels exactly right, or at least thoughtfully employed. The Beatles used it for dramatic purposes, as the music of "Strawberry Fields Forever" and "Helter Skelter" fades and then returns, slightly different. The recording of Buddy Holly's "Not Fade Away" complicates our experience of the insistent lyrics by, playfully, fading away, as does—although with more sorrowful resignation than playfulness—the Bruce Springsteen recording in which he plaintively repeats, "I don't want to fade away."

More importantly, if the power of a good song is to draw listeners into a dream state, the fade can keep them there. The French sociologist Antoine Hennion observes that "pop songs open the doors to dream, lend a voice to what is left unmentioned by ordinary discourse"; defending the fade-out, he notes that "one cannot end a dream, 'full-stop,' just like that." The fade can allow me to believe that a song, even as it ends, continues somewhere—as if the song cannot, in fact, ever finish but exists in some realm even now, after my stereo speakers have gone silent. Harry Nilsson's "Without You" and Al Green's "Have You Been Making Out OK," as they fade, seem merely to be acceding to the arbitrary exigencies of time, which is not a condition of the world from which they come. A poorly written or performed song, recorded formulaically, can fade out and seem merely perfunctory junk, a disposable, unmemorable product of the marketplace; a song that haunts me, that sounds like magic captured by luck in the studio, can, fading out, seem like a bright bit of infinity made briefly incarnate, its vibrations gradually abandoning the air but remaining in me to stay.

"WHITE HOUSE BLUES"

Charlie Poole & the North Carolina Ramblers

1926

As if reluctant to intrude upon the silence, the fiddle seems to hesitate slightly, then begins to scratch away at the melody. The guitar and banjo join in; by the third bar, they're locked together, confident now and cantering. Then Poole begins singing, and things get weird. His voice, dripping with Southernness, is tight, tinny, and wizened. Is he eighty, ninety? Poole is, in fact, thirty-four when this song is recorded in 1926, but his voice seems to be coming from some far, shadowy side of experience, and his words sometimes bump against the border between language and incoherence. He bursts out first with, "Kinley Holland, Kinley squall." Then some phrases arrive that are more intelligible, such as "from Buffalo to Washington." The song's title is "White House Blues." It is possible, with these clues, to begin piecing together the general narrative, which is confirmed with the reference to "Roosevelt in the White House." This is a song about the assassination of William McKinley and the ascension of the vice president, Theodore Roosevelt, to the presidency. An Internet search for the song's lyrics indicates that Poole's first words are actually "McKinley hollered, McKinley squalled."

But, listening to the song, I am not immersed in the story; I am caught up in the busily fingerpicked banjo and guitar and the fiddle, sawing away at the melody, all at a tempo that, as the record nears its end, will speed up to a gallop; I am thinking about the singer, who, only intermittently understandable to me, seems to be singing for someone else. I'm an eavesdropper, as if listening through a closed door. Two pithy couplets do come through clearly. Condensing the story to its metaphysical essence, Poole announces, "Roosevelt's in the White House, he's doing his best. / McKinley's in the graveyard, he's taking his rest." The lines are an understated, vaguely terrifying summary of the situation: not merely of the sudden shift in American political power but, more unsettlingly, of the abrupt, final reversal of circumstance we will all face, as our daily labors give way to permanent repose. In implicit recognition that death—especially sudden, unexpected death—is a horror beyond our power to completely fathom, Poole mordantly offers consolation to the survivors: "Hush up, little children, now don't you fret. / You'll draw a pension at your papa's death."

In Poole's mouth, however, many of the song's words sound like distant cousins of those written on the lyric sheet. "Little children" becomes "widdle chillun." "Carry me back to Washington" sounds more like "gettin' mad to Washington." His reference to Roosevelt "drinking out of a silver cup" sounds equally—or more so—like "hanging out to see what's up." He sings some phrases—"ain't but one thing" and "don't waste your breath"—with only partial completeness, as if he's being poked in the ribs with a stick.

My difficulty deciphering what I am hearing can be credited to Poole's early–twentieth century Appalachian twang, as well as to the low-fidelity 1920s equipment with which the performance was recorded. However, the reasons don't matter as much as the result does. By the end of the record, I am bewitched and mystified, as if I have overheard, coming from a stranger's room, a haunted hymn, the song of some hitherto undocumented religion whose scripture speaks in code so its deepest secrets are concealed from the undeserving.

✦

It makes sense that in the Beatles' "I'm So Tired," John Lennon has to cancel his plane. "You know I can't sleep," he sings. "I cancelled my plane." With such agonizing insomnia, who wouldn't reconsider everything, even his travel plans? For decades, that was my understanding of the lyric. Over the course of forty years, I listened to the record, sang along with it, imagined that unused airline ticket, and empathized with the singer's plight: stuck at home, unable to sleep, unable to fly.

Then one day I heard someone else singing along with the song. "I can't stop my brain," she sang.

"I can't stop my brain"? Yes, of course, that's what he's saying, and has been saying from the start. When I was eleven, I misheard the lyric, and from that time forward I was content not to question that eleven-year-old's ear.

I was also eleven when Hamilton, Joe Frank, and Reynolds' record "Don't Pull Your Love" was a hit. I liked especially the strange, unexpected moment in the song when the singer's wife breaks up with him and takes possession of their pet. "You say you're gonna leave," he sings, "gonna take that big white bird." I could see the woman stomping out of their house for the last time, carrying—with, I imagined, some difficulty—a giant cage containing their bird, perhaps a heron. I supposed she had brought it into the relationship. It took me a couple of years to realize that the subsequent line—"Gonna fly right out

of here"—had been offering me a clue from the beginning:
the bird was a metaphor. The airplane I had placed in the
Beatles song belonged in this one instead.

Around the time I was recognizing my mistake about
"Don't Pull Your Love," a popular song on the radio was
Loudon Wainwright III's "Dead Skunk," which uses the
controlling metaphor of a skunk's rank secretions to meditate upon the problem of air pollution. It took me a few
listens to put together the clues to this deeper level of
meaning: toward the song's end, the lyrics directly refer
to the skunk's scent as "pollution," and, even more of a
giveaway, earlier in the song, Wainwright associates the
smell with an "old factory." Piercing through the lyrics'
comic surface to the serious and urgent theme beneath, I
felt deep and knowing—only thirteen years old but shrewd
enough to recognize the song's environmentalist message.
A few years later, having in the meantime learned the word
"olfactory," I heard the song again, and the old factory
spewing pollution disappeared. The song's subject shrank
to the stink of a dead skunk, that and only that.

During all the time those wrong songs played in my
head, I found no flaw in them, maybe because the mis-
hearings were entirely mine: like responses to a Rorschach
test, they were projections of my own secret system of logic.
Cartoonist Lynda Barry likes to tell a story about "Groo-
vin'" by the Young Rascals, which was a hit when she was
eleven. She was especially enchanted by the line "Life
could be ecstasy, you and me and Leslie." She was curious
about this third person, Leslie: whether Leslie was male or
female and what Leslie was doing showing up so late in the
scene and in the song. Only years later did Barry realize
that the line says not "you and me and Leslie" but "you and
me endlessly." She argues that her version is the superior
one: more surprising and weird and specific and therefore

true—an explosion in the imagination of possibility, not a limply predictable, abstract banality.

In concert, sometimes John Prine would recount an experience he had had with a fan years before at another show. She asked him if he might play his song about a happy enchilada. The request puzzled him, since he'd never, he told her, written a song about any enchilada, let alone a happy one. No, she insisted, he had written the song. When he asked her to quote it, she said, "It's a happy enchilada, and you think you're gonna drown." The riddle was solved: she was thinking of the song that goes "It's a half an inch of water, and you think you're gonna drown." When Prine told that story in later concerts, he made sure, in singing the song, to change one of the choruses so that it included the "happy enchilada." One woman's private understanding of the song had been subsumed, in part, into Prine's own understanding—and that of his other fans.

We are always coauthors of songs we hear; the images and associations they give life to in our minds are ours alone, as are the meanings we attach to the lyrics. Still, from the beginning of my serious interest in popular music, I wanted to know what the true words were. They seemed to be indispensable signals from a wider, more exotic world than mine, signals that, as if by miracle, found their way to my suburban dead-end street and passed through the closed door of my bedroom, where I sat, listening. If a song I loved came on the radio, I reached for my spiral-ring notebook and Flair felt-tip pen and jotted down the words, which always came and went too quickly for me to capture completely. I had to wait for another airing of the song, and then another, to fill in the lyrical blanks.

Nonetheless, no matter how many times I heard them, some words were impossible for me to decipher with confidence. In Todd Rundgren's "I Saw the Light," was he really singing to his girlfriend, "'Cause you couldn't help a mother rest?" In Yes' "Roundabout," what was coming out of the sky—Martians or mountains? In the Rolling Stones' "Tumbling Dice"—I hadn't a clue what was happening in "Tumbling Dice." Luckily, I found help: the neighborhood 7-Eleven store stocked *Song Hits* and *Hit Parader*, monthly magazines that printed lyrics to current popular songs. With the spending money I'd earned from allowances and lawn mowing and pet sitting, I'd been buying 45s and the occasional album. Now I began shelling out thirty-five or fifty cents for these magazines. They were a great help, a real time-saver. Then one month, I read the published lyrics of Elton John's "Rocket Man," which informed me that the song's astronaut was not "burning out his fuse up here alone," as I had thought, but "burning out his fuse of perilon." *Perilon?* I couldn't find the word in my dictionary. I had assumed that these magazines had special access to the official lyrics, but now I wondered if they weren't just doing what I had been doing: giving the songs a fastidious listen and making hopeful guesses. We were all just winging it; we were all in this mystery together.

27 | *Meddling with Perception*

One summer evening, in my twenties, I sat with a woman in an idling car outside of her apartment building. I had recently suffered the abrupt, distressing end of a relationship that had overwhelmed me, that had swept me fully into its twisting winds, a relationship that had been wrong from the start. The woman I had just shared dinner with had troubles of her own: recently divorced, she was suddenly raising, by herself, a young son. As we sat in the front seat, with country music playing on the radio, we were, without saying so, preparing to kiss for the first time, preparing to agree that, instead of dropping her off and driving away alone, I would turn the ignition off and accompany her into her apartment. In that liminal moment, in our hesitation born of nervousness, born of feeling the gravity of turning away from the ghosts of our old partners and toward one another, a man on the radio—soon joined by a harmonizing woman—sang these words:

> You don't look a thing like her,
> And I don't guess I measure up to him.
> Oh, but then, maybe together
> We can get each other over them.

It was Moe Bandy and Becky Hobbs' new hit, "Let's Get Over Them Together." That moment in the car was intense enough as it was; I was fully attentive to it. Yet, as we sat together with our separate, private feelings, a song joined us to announce, Greek chorus–like, what those feelings were, what they amounted to. My memory, afterward, of that moment, and, more importantly, my experience of it then, could not be disentangled from the song's crude belaboring of the obvious—from its admittedly accurate yet reductive explication of what was happening. The cartoonish coincidence of this record, among all possible records, being the one the station played at that moment introduced an element of farce to the proceedings, or maybe laid bare the farce that was there already.

A song can do that: frame your attention to reality in a way that complicates, narrows, or muddles your perceptions. In its indelicate annotating of my experience, that song on the radio both intensified and weakened my sense of what was happening, revealing some sad absurdity in the scene but in doing so directing my thoughts only to that absurdity.

Some songs have specific designs on us: they are eager to evoke a predetermined feeling but, in their eagerness, risk numbing us to it instead. As much as making us surrender to their will, they cause us to think about how we are being coerced to do so. I wonder, for instance, how often Kool and the Gang's "Celebration," with its nonstop exhortations to "celebrate" and to "have a good time," has induced truly unselfconscious revelry. I wonder whether Paul McCartney would have more luck kindling in us a feeling of the wonder of Christmas if he did not continually insist that we are "having a wonderful Christmastime."

More often, no doubt, and more mysteriously, songs affect our perceptions indirectly, covertly. Invited to enter us by our affection for them, they insinuate themselves, over time, patiently, into our beings, until their forms and notions become part of us, ingredients in the roiling soup of our unconscious. By the time, in junior high, I started liking girls, I had been educated by years of hearing Top 40 hits to understand that romantic love involved climbing on rainbows, writing your flawless girlfriend's name across the sky, and, as the earth stopped spinning and each star was extinguished, flying away with her into the infinite. Perhaps that is why, suffering the exquisite agony of my first crush, I felt befuddled, almost betrayed, by having those feelings go unrequited. Something wasn't adding up. I had fallen in love, and my heart was true, which meant the object of my devotion was the only girl in the world worthy of it, and a crucial aspect of that worthiness, as I understood it, was that she felt for me as I did for her. It was painful to discover that I had to wait for her to recognize in her own heart this truth she was somehow managing to ignore.

As I grew up and began having serious, complex relationships, a song—if only for a moment—could recalibrate my perceptions. There might be some tension between us, some misunderstanding left unresolved, but I would hear by chance an early favorite song of ours and feel again a sudden tenderness for my partner; I saw her, and us, as we once had been and maybe still were, even if we had forgotten.

28 | *A Dream We Can Return To*

No matter the centrality to music of math—of whole steps and half steps, eighth notes and quarter notes, beats per measure and notes per chord—the effect of a song cannot be accounted for wholly by the rational mind. As long as it is humans who are making music and humans who are listening, a song's power will derive from the parts of us that operate beyond, or beneath, reason and calculation: emotion, imagination, memory, and even the physical fact of the body.

As we slip under the spell of a song, the rhythm gets us slightly swaying or tapping our knees with our fingertips, then a certain turn of the melody puts a twinge in our chest, and a long-dormant feeling is activated, and our mind is jostled; some memory lurking in a shadowy recess comes into the open. Then a memory from some other time joins it. We are alive in—and to—both the present moment of our listening and the past that brought us to it. Or the song is telling a story or imagining a place, and we imagine along with it. We feel both inside and outside of time, both here and elsewhere, attentive to the dimensions we live in yet freed from their strictures. We are aware of a complex of feelings or thoughts borrowed from—but, in this moment, existing apart from—the flow of normal lived reality: they are a distillation or reconstitution that feels weighty with indefinable import and is inexplicably diverting. We are engaged in a form of dreaming.

A real dream vanishes when we wake. A favorite record is a dream we can return to. We listen to its first notes, knowing where they might lead us, and we go there willingly.

"POWDERFINGER"

Neil Young & Crazy Horse

1979

How it begins: a single, casual strum of a guitar and a simultaneous faraway whistle—the enthusiasm of an audience member. This track was recorded live, and engineers eliminated most of the crowd noise later, but that whistle remains: a signal that something communal is about to happen. Neil Young will be pulling us into his dream.

A second later, we're in it: "Look out, Mama," Young warns, in his high voice, brittle and thin as prairie grass, "there's a white boat comin' up the river." Within fourteen syllables, already a complicated dramatic scene and conflict are presented, but we are so close to the action, and so aligned from the start with the narrow perspective of the character who is singing, that we can understand only so much. This is a story song—although much more song than story; or, maybe more accurately, it is an example of how much of a narrative can be communicated merely musically, without reliance on words.

In "Powderfinger," as in a dream, images blur into one another, and hints and implications refuse to resolve themselves. About what is happening and why, we are given only splinters of information, so we have questions that most stories would answer for us but that this song never will. Who is on that boat? Sailors at war? Law enforcement officials? A criminal gang? The fact that the vessel flies a flag and has a gun and numbers on its side suggests a warship, but there is no certainty about that. And when and where is this taking place, exactly? Because the answers are not provided, they seem not to matter. What matters instead is what the song presents directly: a young man's scattered, panicky thoughts and actions as he is confronted with a sudden threat of death. Danger is coming, and he must react. The song puts us in his head and nervous system, and it keeps us there.

Because this is not a story we are encountering as words on the page, we cannot slow our experience of it or pause, ponder, then return. The fact of its being a song—something unstoppable, moving through time—introduces from the beginning a sense of dread. The inevitability of whatever is to come is present from the first downbeat, and the song and story charge along relentlessly from that moment, with the fierce, firm drumbeat and churning guitars of Crazy Horse—reckless and manic, seeming at risk of careening out of control—pushing us, and the terrified narrator, unavoidably toward the climax. Even as the song hurtles forward, its center holds, signaled most powerfully by a recurring guitar riff: a run of notes that rises and falls and then is cut off by a long, low power chord, as if doom were lurking from the start.

The dread hangs heavy over every line. "I think you'd better call John," the singer says to his mother, and then he adds, with faltering delivery, an understatement: "It don't look like they're here to deliver the mail." Young's timing in this line is almost comic; he pauses, as if in despairing recognition, before the final two words, which he then sings as if swallowing them. At the next line—"And it's less than a mile away"—other members of the band add spookily foreboding background vocals: a wordless, ghostly, "Ooo-ooo-ooh."

The second verse offers a quick litany of the men who, in another circumstance, might be there to defend the homestead but are gone: the young man's father and brother and "Big John." Then an odd thing happens: the narrative, which has been in present tense throughout, shifts unexpectedly to past tense. The character who, in the first line, announces, "Look out, Mama, there's a white boat," now says, "I was wonderin' what to do." We are transported suddenly ahead in time, to a nameless afterward, as if whatever is on the verge of happening has somehow happened already; it is fated.

After this verse, we hear the first of two Young guitar solos, a respite from the action, a moment to breathe. Yet we are not forgetful of the young man's dilemma: the guitar playing is not so much virtuosic—this is no time to show off—as completely genuine, remaining in the emotional frame the song has established, the wailing and ringing notes expressive of the tumult within the character that no words could name.

The singer returns to finish his story. Forced, perhaps too soon, into the role of the family patriarch, he grabs his father's rifle. A bullet from the boat hits the dock, and he raises the rifle to shoot back, but he never has a chance: "Then I saw black and my face splashed in the sky."

Everything happens so quickly here that we experience the chaos of the incomplete. We know too little to make full sense of the narrative and therefore to be comforted by, and maybe complacent in, our understanding. Is the young man's father dead or merely traveling? The father has previously warned, "Red means run, son." Does red refer to the color of the boat's beacon? A uniform? Blood? Why, then, does the son not run? Why does he aim his father's rifle? Does he have no time to escape? The character says he "never stopped to wonder why." Why what, exactly—that he aims the gun? So much is compressed here into so few lines that our understanding remains frustratingly partial, even useless, as if all the song cares to share is the character's bewilderment and terror in the seconds preceding his death. These are the things we do know, or rather feel, in no small part because of Young's vocals—reedy, and sometimes straining and quavery, but always with expressive consequences. His is the voice of someone unnerved and awed by an overwhelming force.

"Powderfinger" seems not to be a story of heroism—of a young man's courageous confrontation with danger. It is a recounting of an early, purposeless death at the hands of a distant, anonymous foe. What can the song say now, at the moment of death, especially when the tale's narrator is the dead man himself? What could he know to tell? He sees "black," and his face ceases to exist—he ceases to exist. The music alone must do the talking now, for the wordless sounds of instruments can express that for which verbal language is insufficient. At this moment of the character's death, Young takes his second guitar solo. What else could he do? As Greil Marcus observes, "Building in any successful rock 'n' roll record is a sense of the power of the singer to say what he or she means, but also a realization that words are inadequate to that task, and the feeling of fulfillment is never as strong as the feeling of frustration . . . and so an instrument takes over. It is a relief: a relief from the failure of language. The thrill is of entering a world where anything can be said, even if no one can know what it means."

After the guitar solo, a final verse—a kind of coda—occurs. The narrator returns, speaking from beyond the grave. Confirming that the cause of his death is not as important as the mere fact of the death itself, his thoughts are not on the larger conflict he got caught up in (we still don't know who was on that boat, or why); what is on his mind instead is that he has been made to "fade away so young / With so much left undone." And then, in a poi-

gnantly understated last line, he introduces us to a character we haven't encountered before: "Remember me to my
love. / I know I'll miss her." This is a reminder of just how
narrowly focused and fragmentary the narrative has been.
We have not been privy to the larger story of which it is a
part: the lives of these characters and their relationships
and problems—that is, almost everything about them that
they might consider important beyond the appearance one
day of a menacing ship on the river.

"Powderfinger" reminds us of inexplicable mysteries by
gesturing toward them, circling around them, or falling
into wordlessness in the face of them. It reminds us how
essentially strange and incompletely knowable our lives are,
and our deaths. As with a dream, its power is in how it
hints at its secrets even while it keeps them.

29 | *The Space Where Singer and Listener Meet*

The cry of a pedal steel guitar, the sprinkling of a few piano notes, and then a voice—wounded, fragile—singing, "You may be sweet and nice / But that won't keep you warm at night."

Why am I taking this personally? Why the heaviness in my heart? I didn't write this song—"Hot Burrito #1" by the Flying Burrito Brothers. I am not the singer; Gram Parsons is. I am not the "you" Parsons addresses. By all rights, I should be considered a stranger to the song, which existed in the world a dozen years before I knew of it, its singer dead a decade before I first heard his voice. What is he to me, or I to him, that I should weep for him? This song's business is not my business. I am an eavesdropper.

Maybe that's the point: I spy on any song from the safety of a concealed location—my own interior. Such eavesdropping is less like overhearing a conversation in the neighboring booth at a restaurant than like stumbling upon it in a dream. Defenseless, I become a party to the song's concerns. I identify with, maybe imagine I am, the singer, finding in the song—or imposing upon it—some worry or wonder or gladness of my own. Personal memories and imaginings, like ghosts frustrated by unfinished business, are awakened by the music and emerge and intertwine, liberated to create and play out a private drama, an enactment of feelings taken from life but at one remove from it, one remove from other people. In our normal, everyday interactions with others, we are armed with wariness. To open ourselves emotionally to them, or themselves to us, is to risk disapproval or misunderstanding. A song, though, offers inspiration and permission to feel—without apology, explanation, or risk. We can listen as many times as we wish, in as many ways as we wish. The song will never know we are there.

Songs can be airy enough to absorb almost any private association we bring to them. They are "like smoke," says Tom Waits. "Songs aren't necessarily verbatim chronicles or necessarily journal entries . . . . [U]sually a song will remind you of something, it will take you back somewhere and make you think of somebody or someplace. They're like touchstones, or a mist."

As the dreamer in sleep is lured to do, the listener in thrall to a seductive song finds herself traveling anywhere, becoming anyone. I am not in the habit of defending acts of senseless murder, but, as I listen to "Folsom Prison Blues," my imagination—game for any challenge—allows me to sympathize with the singer who "shot a man in Reno / Just to watch him die." As I listen to "Long Black Veil," I find no difficulty in becoming a moldering corpse: the man executed for a crime he did not commit who remained silent in the courtroom but now sings his tale from the grave.

The pained, betrayed singer of "Hot Burrito #1" is addressing a woman who has found delight in another man's arms after learning how to love in his, but the woman doesn't answer; she isn't there. We, as listeners, are more present than she is. We, in our dream, encounter the singer in his. As sociologist Antoine Hennion writes, "The frequent use of the direct style where, for example, the 'I' addresses itself to the 'you,' even though it is obvious from the lyrics that the 'you' in question is far away, instantly gives the song the form of a fantasy, of a daydream." In a way, then, the first important listener to the singer's complaint is the singer himself, as if he is rehearsing in private, in the safety of his own mind, what he would say out loud if he had the chance or nerve. The second listener is any one of us who cares to listen to his complaint, any stranger who might take on that complaint as his or her own.

That bond between singer and listener is a gift, delivered across time and space, from the musician who records a song to the person who plays the record: the gift of a reminder of our enduring human connection. I never met Gram Parsons—or Levi Stubbs or Al Green or Billie Holiday—but to hear their songs is to feel that I understand a part of them, and they of me. It does not matter if this is true; their music convinces me that it is.

Proust wrote before the ubiquity of recorded music; his scenes involving music are set in concert halls and at soirées in private homes. He created characters who understand how music can make us feel a profound connection to a stranger, even a stranger who, years ago, went to his grave. When music and a listener's imagination meet, the two forces inhabit a shared space in which two lives, that of the composer or performer and that of the listener, seem to meld. In *Swann's Way*, when Swann, at a concert, is emotionally transported by hearing his loved little phrase of Vinteuil's, his feelings expand beyond the pain of his own sorrow to sympathy for the composer's: "[F]or the first time Swann's thoughts turned with a stab of pity and tenderness to Vinteuil, to that unknown, sublime brother who must also have suffered so; what must his life have been like? From the depths of what sorrows had he drawn that godlike strength, that unlimited power to create?"

In *The Captive*, Proust's narrator recognizes how Vinteuil's music somehow contains the man who wrote it: "Vinteuil had been dead for many years; but in the sound of these instruments which he had animated, it had been given him to prolong, for an unlimited time, a part at least of his life."

Thirty years ago, I found myself at the kitchen table of an accomplished violinist, someone who had devoted her life to sounding, with precision and feeling, the arrangements of notes created by Beethoven, Mendelssohn, and Brahms. Her vocation, it struck me suddenly, must contain a deep vein of generosity and humility. Through her playing, the imaginings of the long dead were kept alive, given yet another chance to enter the feelings and imaginings of listeners. She was a necessary emissary, bringing from the past news that is still vital in the present. She and Mozart were talking with each other across centuries, and both of them were talking to us.

No, she told me. She didn't think of it that way. She didn't think I was right. I still think I was.

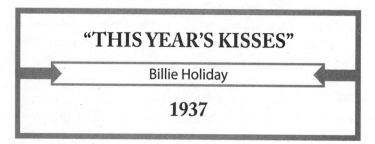

"THIS YEAR'S KISSES"

Billie Holiday

1937

To listen to this record is to overhear quiet, natural, charged talk among friends. The subject of the conversation is sorrowful, but the melancholy is mixed with convivial spirits into an alloy that feels something like resilience, even joy. Irving Berlin's lyrics suggest dejection, but, in this performance, the singer's sad state is less a reason for lamenting than an occasion for finding cheer in camaraderie, and in music itself.

The tune begins with a quick four-bar introduction by Teddy Wilson on piano, and then Lester Young, on tenor sax, takes a twenty-eight-bar chorus: unhurried and sure, shimmering with personality, establishing the melody while messing with it at its edges, stamping the song immediately with a tone of easy, playful intimacy. The lyric we are about to hear concerns love gone wrong, or love not quite right, but, before this solo is done, it is already too late for the song ever to get maudlin. Young ends his solo with a little flutter of notes that fades modestly away, making room for Holiday, who sings, like a shy person beguiled into speech by feeling, "This year's crop of kisses / Don't seem as sweet to me." Her casual swing gives the words the bittersweet tone of someone wounded but resigned to it, someone perhaps already getting over it because she's found a way to sing of it.

As she continues, bass, drums, and guitar buoy her while Wilson's piano adds understated flourishes—and Buck Clayton's trumpet will make some lovely assertions in the record's final bars. In the meantime, though, it is Young who seems to understand, and even anticipate, Holiday's every word. He responds, as if from just behind her, with his saxophone whispering patient little reassurances and affirmations between and beneath her words. Holiday's wistful voice hovers, slightly detached from the beat, a balloon riding a light breeze, while Young floats behind her, rising when she rises, veering when she veers. They are talking with one another, finishing each other's thoughts, intertwining, playing out an intimate drama, and we are listening in.

The story the lyrics tell is of a woman, amid new love, pining for an old one, but that former lover is not nearly as important a character as the saxophone that accompanies Holiday as she sings. The central drama the performance enacts might be an entirely internal one, the saxophone and voice so aligned that they could be two parts of the singer in conversation. The song enters us invisibly, through the ears, acting within us in an intimate way that staged drama, with its physicality—its sets and lights and separate human bodies—cannot.

"This Year's Kisses" is about a type of romantic trouble so familiar it calcified early into a Tin Pan Alley cliché. But when Billie Holiday sings the song, bringing to it her entire self, alert to the moment, the lyrics' pained yearning comes through simultaneously with her delight in singing about it: in adding the instrument of her voice to this swinging conversation among musical equals. This immediacy, this aliveness to feeling, brings alive in me a feeling that otherwise lies buried, dormant. Holiday's voice calls out, and Lester Young responds, as if speaking for an unseen part of her—for an unseen part of any of us: the inscrutable emotion that precedes and gives rise to speech. He is that which comes before words, having its say.

Part Four
The World in the Song

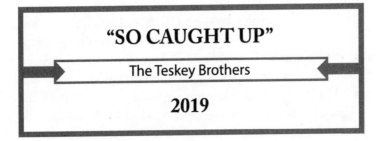

"SO CAUGHT UP"

The Teskey Brothers

2019

I'm in the car listening to an FM rock station, itchy finger ready to punch the button; experience has taught me to doubt that I'll want to hear whatever song comes next. Then a bass note and almost simultaneous cymbal crash announce the tune—something I've never heard before; clinking piano notes accentuate the languid, loping beat, and a pretty guitar lick—a swift slide between notes, verging on cute—appears once, then recurs in each bar. What is this? I have no desire to change the station.

Vocals are sure to enter soon; they could send me scurrying. But a soulful, whiskey-and-honey voice moans, "I'm so caught up, I'm so caught up on you," and I do not doubt the singer, nor do I doubt that I'll be sticking around for the whole song. So far, it is pure pleasure; each element of this tuneful record, one after the other—the insistently percussive piano, the winsome guitar, the torrid singing, and now (another thing!) some sweetly *ooh-ooh*-ing background vocals, and now (another!) a horn section gliding into the tune with a smooth, four-note, descending phrase—is like a shot of sugar. Wait; for goodness sake: are those pizzicato strings?

This sounds like a lost soul record from the sixties or seventies, something from Muscle Shoals or Stax. The Dells? The Dramatics? I realize that my delight, as I am hearing this song for the first time, is born largely of how familiar it sounds. The singer isn't Otis Redding, but he could be his cousin; he isn't Wilson Pickett, but he might have forged his style by listening a thousand times to Pickett's "I Found a Love." The tap-tap-tapping pianist and minimalist guitarist might as well be Booker T. Jones and Steve Cropper, teleported into the record from 1963 and Redding's "Pain in My Heart." If—as the radio station playing it is an indication—this is a recent record, the bassist I hear can't be Duck Dunn but only because Duck Dunn is dead.

As the song continues into the verses and bridge, the lyrics remain spare and not particularly inventive—familiar complaints about the failure to forget a lost love—but the absence of linguistic flair does not matter. The words are mere scaffolding around which the impassioned vocals wind, climbing toward pangs of yearning, dipping into shrugs of resignation. Meanwhile, hooks at every turn. If it were 1972, this 45 might be found in the drugstore racks next to Bobby Womack, the Staple Singers, and Billy Paul.

Is this classic soul or a reference to classic soul? How much of my happy attention to the song is due to its musical enticements, and how much to the riddles it raises: who the group is, when the tune was recorded, and—if it was recorded recently—why it sounds as though it is fifty years old? The whole song reminds me of things that it isn't, of ghost songs that haunt it. In the meantime, whatever it actually is, in itself, is not bad: not merely homage, parody, or pastiche. When I hear the song again, and then again, how much of the pleasure will remain, even deepen? Am I hearing exhumation or resurrection?

✦

Music is an ocean of correspondences. Like a wave, a song laps at the edge of our consciousness, its particles sparkling with hints of elsewhere, of other songs whose musical gestures it has gathered, reshaped, and taken into itself. I suspect that, whether we take conscious note of them or not, these allusions and borrowings contribute to a song's power over us. They signal that the song is part of something more vast than itself: an ongoing conversation that songs have been having for a long time with one another and that we have been having for a long time with ourselves. Some of what a song shares with other songs is unavoidable, characteristics of form that make us call it a song to begin with. Other borrowings are more direct and pointed: an allusive melodic line or riff or lyric or vocal timbre that can cause us, while listening to a record, to recall another song and suddenly hear the two as being in dialogue with each other.

But the process of transplanting an element of one song into another is a delicate one and, with the wrong intentions, can disenchant a listener, in the way magic can fail for those not willing to suspend their disbelief in it. There is a fine and perhaps indefinable line between homage and theft, between an exhilarating act of an expansive, associative imagination and a dispiriting act of mere fancy that filches the fire of another record to give life to that which would otherwise be dead. A musical borrowing that seems an act of generosity, humility, and playfulness—of openness to a song's possibilities—can bewitch me, while an allusion that seems inspired merely by commercial considerations, one that seems to be a clumsy, cynical shortcut around the need for invention and artistry, puts me on the defensive, as though I have answered the phone and found myself listening to a honey-tongued telemarketer.

Hip-hop, with its use of sampling, is built on excavation of the musical past; a bass riff or drum break from a forty-year-old record can become the foundation of an invigorating new piece of music that, in recontextualizing the sampled fragment of sound, both creates something new and makes us listen with fresh ears to the record that is its source. Hip-hop might have brought into the contemporary mainstream of popular music the conscious act of musical borrowing, but songs have always been caught in the act of thinking, or dreaming, about other songs. When they do, they can deepen the listener's dream: the sound we recognize from elsewhere resonates with tones and implications we absorbed into ourselves long ago, and those things rise from within us to complicate our emotional experience of the new song. In Nina Simone's version of Rodgers and Hart's "Little Girl Blue," she interpolates, in a recurring piano figure, the melody of "Good King Wenceslas," a tune we associate with the Christmas season. The interplay of the two melodies—one for a song about a lonely woman yearning for love, one for a song about a charitable saint—introduces, into an otherwise secular love song, a suggestion of the mythic and sacred. The poignancy of the lyrics' depiction of human isolation is complicated by the melodic association with the idea of humans' divine connections to one another.

A less suggestive borrowing occurs when the Beach Boys sing "Surfin' USA" to the melody of Chuck Berry's "Sweet Little Sixteen"—it makes for an energetic record but one not wholly loyal to a vision of its own; the presence of Berry's melody feels more like outright theft than reimagining. An opposite approach, one that makes reliance on the melody of an old song an organic ingredient in the new one, can be heard in Neil Young's "Borrowed Tune." Starting with the title, he admits his plagiarism, and it becomes part of the story he tells. To the tune of the Rolling Stones' "Lady Jane," Young sings, "I'm singing this borrowed tune / I took from the Rolling Stones. / Alone in this empty room, / Too wasted to write my own." His reliance on the Stones melody, and his direct contemplation of this fact, makes the song all the more persuasive as a dramatization of imaginative detachment and inertia.

The slow, one-hesitant-step-at-a-time quality of the Jagger and Richards melody feels right, too, for the introspectiveness of Young's lyric. Any number of components of a familiar song can do that: insinuate into a new tune a certain feeling or association that enriches the song's implications. A court found George Harrison guilty of copyright infringement for employing, in "My Sweet Lord," a melody similar to that in the Chiffons hit "He's So Fine," even though the judge acknowledged that Harrison probably copied the melody "unconsciously." If so, Harrison's unconscious had its reasons, and the unconscious of any listener familiar with both songs might sense those reasons, too. Both "He's So Fine" and "My Sweet Lord" are about adoration and desire; in the former tune, the singer adores a handsome boy with wavy hair and yearns to make him her own, so much so that she is willing to wait forever. In the latter tune, the singer adores his "Lord," whom he yearns to "see" and "be with," even while he recognizes that waiting for such a union "takes so long." In setting his lyrics to a melody almost identical to the one in the older song, Harrison might have been inspired by associations, buried in his unconscious, between that particular rousing melody and the experience of joyful anticipation of union with an idealized beloved.

Again and again, some detail in a song reminds me of another song, and that fact can't be shaken loose from my experience of the record. For a few notes, Steely Dan's

"Barrytown" seems to align itself with the tune of "When You Wish Upon a Star," and the lyrics feel all the more sardonic for being so far from what Jiminy Cricket might ever croon. In the Raspberries' "Go All the Way," the repeated imperative "Come on," sung as a call and response, makes the song a descendant of the Beatles' "Please Please Me." The allusion allows me to experience the tune as a winking homage to the masters but also as an audacious updating of them: while John Lennon, with coy discretion, says "please" as he pleads with his girlfriend, ambiguously, merely to "please" him, Eric Carmen reports that his girlfriend says "please" as she actually begs him to take her completely.

Lennon himself made a habit of alluding to the rock and rollers who preceded him, beginning the song "Come Together" with a reference to a Chuck Berry lyric and "Run for Your Life" with a direct quote from Elvis Presley's "Baby Let's Play House." One of Elvis' own hits, "Love Me Tender," is set to the melody of the Civil War–era tune "Aura Lee." In the bridge section of "The Tears of a Clown," as Smokey Robinson sings of hiding his painful feelings behind a smile, the Miracles call out behind him, "The Great Pretender!," alluding to the Platters hit on a similar theme of a dozen years before. In the Jackson Five's 1970 song "I'll Be There," Michael Jackson tips his cap to the similarly titled Four Tops hit "Reach Out, I'll Be There," quoting one of its lines as he shouts, toward the song's end, "Just look over your shoulders, honey!"

Such nodding by songs to other songs happens over and over, as if each, washing ashore at the ocean's edge, arrives not merely as itself but as a reminder of the deep, vast waters it has been orphaned from.

However, not all musical allusions seem organic to a song's imaginative vision and thus engage my own imagination; some seem cynical or complacent, inspired by commercial considerations or by unexamined allegiance to whatever musical sounds happen to be popular at the moment. In some songs, the borrowings are so overt as to carry with them a hint of desperation, even cravenness, the result being that the music sounds distant and canned—fun, perhaps, in its way, but offering only surface-level pleasures. In the 1960s, for instance, the guitar-powered, harmonizing bands of the British Invasion brought an urgent, joyful, raw energy to the pop charts, but it did not take long for the sound, say, of the latest Beatles hit to transmute into the sound of the latest offering by the Monkees, a group of actors cast in a television series about a band of charming, Beatles-like madcaps. In the first Monkees single, "Last Train to Clarksville," released in August 1966, it is difficult not to hear—in the main guitar riff, the vocal harmonies, and the stop-and-start quality of the arrangement—the sound of the Beatles' "Paperback Writer," which had been a hit two months earlier. By the following spring, a record such as the Five Americans' "Western Union"—with its rapid, wordless vocal break *duh-duh-duh-duh-duh, duh-duh-duh-duh-duh* sounding very much like Micky Dolenz' *doo-doo-doo-doo-doo-doo-doo-doo* in "Last Train to Clarksville"—seems like the offspring of the Monkees as much as of the Beatles.

In 1965, Barry McGuire's "Eve of Destruction"—its lyrics written by an eighteen-year-old, P. F. Sloan—sounds, indeed, like something written by an eighteen-year-old, particularly one who has been listening to a lot of Bob Dylan records. With its meticulous litany of complaints about oppression, hatred, violence, and hypocrisy, the song has behind it what Dylan called his "finger-pointing songs," such as "The Times They Are A-Changin'," as well as his apocalyptic-symbolist narrative "A Hard Rain's A-Gonna Fall." Dylan himself is famously a borrower—or, to some, thief—of others' musical ideas, and the lyric structure of

"A Hard Rain's A-Gonna Fall" is itself based on the centuries-old English ballad "Lord Randall." However, Barry McGuire's recording of "Eve of Destruction" refers to its immediate progenitor so thoroughly as to sound close to parody: it contains a Dylanesque gruff, unpolished vocal and harmonica solo, lyrics weighty with ominous warnings, and even dropped final *g* sounds, as in *explodin'* and *loadin'*. With so many ingredients familiar from Dylan performances baked into a song that snarls, "You don't believe we're on the eve of destruction," I'm not convinced that even the song believes it. The possibility of my hearing "Eve of Destruction" as an earnest, heartfelt warning is undermined by my hunch that it is cashing in on a cultural moment.

Like any kind of art, music stays alive by staying in motion, changing as it takes into itself new ideas and forms. However, when those ideas and forms seem entirely secondhand, not reimagined, the effect is enervation. There are only a few small steps yet a million miles between Little Richard's "Tutti Frutti" and Pat Boone's "Tutti Frutti," between the Sex Pistols' "Anarchy in the U.K." and the Knack's "My Sharona," and between Hank Williams and whatever T-shirted hunk in a cowboy hat currently rides high on the country charts.

One kind of unpersuasive borrowing manifests itself in bathos: something that is costumed as feeling but gives off a whiff of the ridiculous or distasteful. Consider "Rock and Roll Heaven," a 1974 hit by the Righteous Brothers. The song presents itself as a celebration of great, recently deceased musicians, honoring them by alluding to their work, but what it knows and feels about that work seems entirely superficial. The dead musicians—Jimi Hendrix, Janis Joplin, Otis Redding, Jim Morrison, Jim Croce, and Bobby Darin—appear once each in the song, then disappear, but not before we are given a single fact to associate with them, as if that fact is sufficient to communicate something essential about them. We are typically presented with the title of their most famous song, such as "The Dock of the Bay," "Light My Fire," and "Mack the Knife." Of Croce's biggest hit, "Bad, Bad Leroy Brown," the lyrics remind us only that he "touched us" with it. "Bad, Bad Leroy Brown" may be many things—playful, cartoonishly funny, catchy—but calling it touching does not make it so. Combined with the chorus' banal notion that the great dead may be playing in a "hell of a band" in "rock and roll heaven," such vacuities make the lyric feel factory-made, not heartfelt. The song seems less to honor its dead musicians than to exploit them.

It is as if, in knowing too well, too soon, the feelings it wishes to evoke and its strategy of alluding to other songs to make that happen, "Rock and Roll Heaven" extinguishes those feelings. For a musical borrowing to enrich a song, not cheapen it, perhaps the song must seem only vaguely aware of that borrowing, even surprised by it. The tune must be so busy, musically and imaginatively, with all that it is doing on its own that the melodic line or riff or lyric fragment that suddenly appears from elsewhere might as well have leapt into the song on its own because it had no choice; it knew it belonged there.

31 | *The Unnameable Bigger Thing*
—Songs as Metonyms

A song worth returning to seems—as perhaps any memorable work of art does—a metonym. It is a compact, self-contained thing that grows large with implication; we direct our attention to it, even as it is pointing elsewhere. *Metonymy* comes from the Greek *metonymia*, meaning "change of name"—a metonym refers to something indirectly by naming another thing we associate with it. To speak of "Wall Street" or "Hollywood" is to speak not just of literal places but of entire industries and economic systems we associate with those places. When Bessie Smith moans "Empty Bed Blues," her lament is not about her bed so much as about the thrilling but untrustworthy lover who lately lay there with her. When Malvina Reynolds pokes fun at identical "little boxes" on the hillside, she evokes not just unlovely, standardized suburban architecture but unlovely, standardized measures of value and the stultification of imagination. When Bob Dylan sings of a place called "Desolation Row," he is referring to—oh, who knows?—anything, everything.

The metonymic quality of a song is present not merely in the rhetorical strategy of the lyrics. It is present in all that is beyond or beneath the words: the melody, harmony, and rhythm, as well as the timbre of everything—the singer's voice and the instruments, each of which might contribute an important but incompletely definable emotional connotation. As a complex of implications, the song, in our mind, summons something larger than itself, something uncontained and only vaguely nameable yet real, recognizable, and felt: a wild, shape-shifting creature the tip of whose tail the music helps us grasp, briefly, before it slips away.

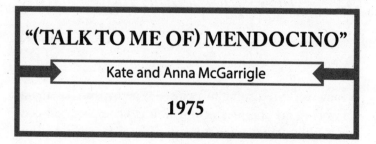

"(TALK TO ME OF) MENDOCINO"

Kate and Anna McGarrigle

1975

From the beginning, we are on the move—not through a story but through a landscape. "I bid farewell to the state of old New York," Kate sings: we are in a specific location but are already traveling away from it. The song will cause us to journey—swiftly, in the way only the imagination can— from one coast to the other, from New York to California, from despondency to hope, from mutability to the promise of permanence.

New York itself, we learn, is but a stop along the singer's larger journey; it is her "home away from home," the place she first roamed to, the place she came of age. It is the place that has wounded her and made her yearn to escape. The sorrow beneath this longing is underscored by the song's instrumentation: the rich, sonorous piano and low, discreet accordion accompaniment.

Still, amid this melancholy, there is wit, if only in the ingenuity of the language. In the second verse, a lovely, unlikely rhyme appears:

> And the trees grow high in New York State
> And they shine like gold in autumn.
> Never had the blues from whence I came
> But in New York State I caught 'em.

In that "autumn/caught 'em" rhyme is a hint of world-weary wryness; one contracts the blues, evidently, by chance, as one does a contagion. The play with colors—the "gold" giving way to "blues"—also shows a mind, even in the midst of grief, still imaginatively alive to possibility and complexity, as does the presence of the autumn leaves: shining like precious gold yet, in that very color, evincing the inevitability of change and loss. Midway through this verse, a plaintive violin enters, making more emphatic the singer's sadness. Still, the lyrics' linguistic deftness shimmers with the kind of implicit joy—or at least hope—involved in the making of a beautiful, memorable thing.

This beautiful thing, this song, allows us to imagine, along with the singer, a place in which her sorrows will dissolve. "Talk to me of Mendocino," Kate sings, with her sister Anna harmonizing. She imagines already that she can hear the sounds of the Pacific, and we hear them, too, as three muffled drumbeats suggest waves collapsing upon the shore.

Then suddenly we seem to be truly heading West. The orchestral accompaniment swells, and the two sisters sing in unison, "And it's on to South Bend, Indiana, / Flat out on the western plain," the song's yearning bursting into a rush of movement, a propulsive act of imagining that makes us "rise up over the Rockies and down on into California, / Out to where but the rocks remain." In a single verse—with only a handful of geographical references signifying the breadth of a nation—we traverse a continent.

The tall trees of New York vanish, replaced by the even taller trees of Northern California. Instead of being surrounded by the dying leaves of autumn, the singer will live with the sturdy, unchanging Redwoods, over which she will watch the sun rise. "I'll rise with it till I rise no more," she proclaims, in a promise to end her journeying at last.

If only in her mind, she has escaped to Mendocino, and the song has carried us there with her. By its end, "(Talk to Me of) Mendocino" has taken us from the East Coast to the West, from the blues to the evergreens, from sorrow to relief, all of this in three minutes and a single sweeping motion of the imagination.

✦

I was on Interstate 40, but, because I was motoring west through Gallup, New Mexico, it was "Route 66" I was humming.

Visiting Chicago for the first time, I turned a corner and found myself not just on State Street but, I sang to myself, on "State Street, that great street."

Must one be born and raised in Winslow, Arizona, not to pause before crossing one of its intersections and think, "I'm standing on a corner in Winslow, Arizona"?

Are the dozens of people, strangers to one another, ambling down Penny Lane or Abbey Road at any given moment all thinking generally the same thing?

Having moved to Alabama and not liked it, I thought maybe I should reconsider because the song "Stars Fell on Alabama" made me think I was missing something.

If I'm going to San Francisco, I imagine wearing flowers in my hair.

Driving toward Los Angeles, a hundred miles away, I begin to fight off the songs: "99 miles from L.A., I want you, I need you. . . . L.A. is a great big freeway, put a hundred down and buy a car. . . . If I can just get off of that L.A. freeway . . . . Santa Monica Boulevard (we love it!), Sixth Street!"

Have people visiting Paris in April felt—because they have heard the song "April in Paris"—an unnecessary chill and loneliness?

Spending a summer month in Saratoga, I visit the racetrack and look at the horses, the dirt, the stands, and the crowd, but I do so doubtfully. It is all real—I know that—but I can't help thinking of it as a stage set for the Carly Simon song that I can't shake from my head. ("I hear you flew up to Saratoga / And your horse naturally won.")

In Greenwich Village, walking Fourth Street, I find myself snarling, "You've got a lot of nerve . . . ."

Can autumn in New York ever seem as richly like autumn in New York as autumn in New York in "Autumn in New York"?

✦

Once, I sat at a conference room table with several other professors in a committee meeting. Concerning a project we were contemplating for which we needed more information, someone suggested that we ask Alex, another faculty member, about it. "Yes," I said. Then, with a lifted eyebrow, I added—aiming for Grace Slick's steady tempo and deadpan tone—"Go ask Alex. I think he'll know."

No one grinned. No one groaned. No one in any way confessed to having caught the Jefferson Airplane allusion. *No one else was in my head.* No one else, I was reminded again, was in my life. A mind full of music can do that: provide the soundtrack to a person's separateness—even nourish that separateness.

A couple of decades ago, chatting with a graduate student, someone in his twenties, I asked what he had done during spring break. "I went back to Ohio," he said.

Delighted that chance was letting the two of us slip briefly, as one, into the lyrics of a Pretenders song, I replied, "And your city was gone?"

His face went blank. "What?"

I had assumed the song was well known enough to be recognized at least by someone who had grown up in Ohio, but he had never heard of Chrissie Hynde's elegy for Akron.

It works the other way, too. I teach poetry writing, and the more years that pass, the more frequent are the occasions when a student poem puzzles me because it alludes to music of which I am ignorant—a Beyoncé or Adele or Kanye West song, maybe.

If someone catches one of my own musical allusions, I feel comforted: confirmed as part of a community—as when, being interviewed once for a job, I explained my reasons for wishing to leave my current position by quoting a Talking Heads song ("My God, what have I done?") and the two people interviewing me smiled and nodded appreciatively.

I find it safest, though, to direct my musical references to infants. When our first son, Milo, was born, a delivery room nurse wiped him down, swaddled him, and handed him to me. I held him to my chest, bent my head toward his little face, and beneath my breath cooed what I'd been cooing to him for months as he grew within the womb: "Milo row your boat ashore, halle-l-u-u-u-jah." He showed no signs of recognition, but, as he was only minutes old, I forgave him that. Upon the arrival of Milo's little brother, Oliver, I thought often of the stage musical that goes by his name, and I took to chirping jollily to him, in a cartoonish Cockney accent, "Consider yourself at home, consider yourself one of the family."

I can't help myself. Songs from deep in memory, transformed, erupt into consciousness as accompaniment to my experience, whatever that experience might be. Songs provide ready-made structures that give imaginative shape to reality. That shape might intensify my connection to a moment; then again, it might diminish that connection as I impose upon the moment a feeling or idea imported randomly from elsewhere.

When, as in that faculty meeting, I am among other people and a phrase from a song rises in my mind and I utter it aloud and it fails, the allusion not taking hold, falling at my feet with a whimper, I feel suddenly aware of what might be my permanent condition: whatever reality I am in, I am in it alone.

32 | A World Full of Music

A soundtrack plays within me through the day, a shuffle of fragments: the chorus of one song, the bridge of another, the emphatically melodic bass line of a third—the music low, unobtrusive, but there; it retreats when I answer the phone or open the front door to shoo an insistent solicitor from my porch, but otherwise a tune seems always to be moving through my mind, even now as I write these words, the music rising in volume when, uncertain what to write next, I lift my fingers from the keyboard and pause, some melody accompanying my rumination, maybe a song I heard earlier today, maybe an earworm by a literate indie rock band I've been listening to this month or "Sugar Sugar" by the Archies (no doubt because it was alluded to in a magazine article I read three days ago), and then that tune gives way, perhaps because of the similarly jaunty tempo, to "If I Only Had a Brain," and then suddenly "Polka Dots and Moonbeams," the Sarah Vaughan version, slips in, even as it did last night, when, sinking into sleep, I gave myself over to its delicate slow dancing.

I suspect this is common, an ever-ready music being present in the mind, planted there by experience and then blossoming into a complement to, or even commentary on, our further experience. The music operates as a low-level waking dream, the suggestion of some inarticulable order, some sense, our minds are making of reality. Cheryl Strayed, in her memoir, *Wild*, recounts becoming aware of the ever-present soup of songs bubbling up into her consciousness. During a three-month-long solitary hike along the Pacific Crest Trail, she discovered that she had unwit-

tingly brought with her, for companionship, a lifetime's
worth of tunes:

> When I wasn't internally grumbling about my
> physical state, I found my mind playing and
> replaying scraps of songs and jingles in an eternal,
> nonsensical loop, as if there were a mix-tape radio
> station in my head. Up against the silence, my brain
> answered back with fragmented lines from tunes
> I'd heard over the course of my life . . . .

The outside world, though, has its own music, a
soundtrack that often competes with—and at other times
blissfully joins—the soundtrack within me. It is difficult
to leave the house and not encounter songs: the *bohm bohm
bohm* of a bass-heavy rap track convulsing a car, all its windows down, pulling up alongside mine at a stoplight; the
familiar, seductive, contained flame of an old Peggy Lee
song playing in the coffee shop; a procession of the latest
smooth R&B hits winding through the hair salon.

My mood is often determined by whether such music
feels like a companion to, or an antagonist to, the music
I carry inside me. I was raised in the Catholic Church, in
the sixties and early seventies, in the wake of the Second
Vatican Council, so I have only the vaguest memory of
Mass as a darkly cryptic ritual, the priest with his back to
the congregation, chanting in Latin. Instead, I remember
the pop music: the weekly "guitar Mass," featuring an
ensemble of five or six parishioners who gathered at key
moments near the altar rail and, Peter, Paul, and Mary–like,
strummed and harmonized their way through tunes closer
to those in *Godspell* and *Jesus Christ Superstar* than those
in the traditional hymnal. Whenever I was in church, I
generally found it difficult to focus; week by week, when I

was ten, eleven, and twelve, feeling more and more certain that I was not a believer, I felt a lessening investment in the rituals I was participating in: the kneeling and praying, the professing of the creed, the closing of my mouth upon the Communion wafer melting on my tongue. The Mass was an hour of discomfort, of waiting for it to be finished. But I liked the guitars. They were present, no doubt, to make the Mass feel personal and relevant, to summon the sense of intimacy and celebration that people feel, outside of church, when listening to secular songs. The guitar group sang tender, easy paeans to charity and fellowship: "They'll Know We Are Christians by Our Love," "Joy Is Like the Rain," "Here We Are." I don't remember the songs making me feel closer to the Lord, but I do remember them making me feel less uncomfortable sitting in the pew, because they were not so far removed from the music that was already playing in my head; the songs were structurally, melodically, and linguistically closer to those I listened to on the radio than to the organ-accompanied dusty hymns we might otherwise have been mumbling. Still, these were church songs; they didn't let me forget where I was.

However, when the group sang "Get Together," which I knew from the Youngbloods' hit version, I felt suddenly at ease, ears and mind unresistant, fully open. Here was a tune whose religious connotations I had never particularly noticed, a rock song that I had heard often on the radio and had sung along to, had even sung to myself in private. When suddenly "Get Together" was filling the church, just as it had often filled my head, I was cast back into my life, into myself, recalling the record's big, ripply electric guitar chords, and a joy came over me, not because the music was turning me toward God but because it was turning itself toward me.

Occasions of communal singing are opportunities to discover your place in, or degree of closeness to, a community. At a sporting event, when the arena thunders with the sound of Queen's "We Will Rock You," maybe you stomp along deliriously, unselfconsciously, or maybe you sit wincing. At a birthday party, maybe you're the one who boldly, alone, begins singing the "Happy Birthday" song, implicitly choosing the key for everyone else, or maybe you're the one who comes in a measure late, quietly, and then partially lip-synchs the lyrics.

I once attended a small academic conference in a seaside town in Norway. One evening, after a day in conference rooms listening to lectures and panel discussions, twenty or so of us professors and writers traveled by boat to a tiny nearby harbor island, to dine in a rustic old boat house surrounded by tall pines and spruce. After dessert and coffee, as we sat chatting at our long, rough-hewn wooden tables, the late-summer darkness falling outside, someone pulled out an acoustic guitar. Clutches of mimeographed lyrics suddenly appeared before us. We would be singing.

A friend and I—the only two Americans in the group, surrounded by Norwegians—perused the lyrics, then looked at each other with raised eyebrows. The songs were all earnest mid-sixties English-language folk-pop hits, lyrics that I could not imagine, at that late date, early in the twenty-first century, singing without irony: Chad and Jeremy's "A Summer Song," Simon and Garfunkel's "Scarborough Fair," Bobby Darin's "If I Were a Carpenter." As song gave way to song, and my friend and I gamely sang along, I was struck by how serious and ingenuous our Scandinavian companions were. They seemed to find nothing odd or anachronistic about this ritual but sang full-throatedly, sincerely, finding vitality in tunes that I had long since judged moribund. Leaning toward me, my friend grinned and whispered that we might shake things up by singing something by the Clash. Whatever was happening in that boathouse was not mine to understand; I could not mock it. Thrown into relief by those unpretentious Norwegians, I felt pompous and small, possessor of a pointless mordancy.

A reliable method of assessing your musical tastes—of sensing the dividing line between music that pleases and music that annoys—is to be stuck in a room in which songs chosen by a stranger are playing. When I moved to a town in the Deep South, I made an appointment with a dentist who came highly recommended. As I settled back in the exam room chair, a familiar kind of charmless but innocuous lightweight pop music was being piped into the room, although I did not recognize the song. Then the cheerful dental hygienist swung her tray of metal implements toward me, and the singer began praising his lord and savior. For the next hour, I listened to one song after another celebrate the power of Jesus in my life. When well-dressed people gripping Bibles and pamphlets appear smiling at my door, I tell them I believe religion is a private matter and send them away. On my back, with sharp tools in my mouth prodding and scraping, I felt ambushed and impotent: an incapacitated target for proselytizing. The music I was hearing did not converse with the music in my mind; it bullied it into submission. I felt an intense appreciation then for my previous dentist in another town, who encouraged his patients to choose a CD from hundreds he offered and then listen to it through headphones as they lay in the chair. In that dentist's office, with my own music entering my ears, I was in his chair but still serenely in my life.

In retail establishments, music might act as aural wallpaper—background noise that I can half listen to or tune out—or it might slyly, surreptitiously, encourage me to spend. The right music might temper a surly mood and make me vulnerable to the merchandise's glittering allure, or a shrewdly chosen mix of classical or jazz pieces might prey on my covert desire to feel sophisticated, worthy of the store. When I get my hair cut at the local outlet of a low-cost nationwide chain salon, I am usually made to listen to contemporary hit radio: formulaic hip-hop–inspired dance tracks and hyperbolically melismatic female singers. Once, however, I was the lone customer in the store, a single stylist was on duty, and she was playing, on a portable tape deck, a homemade mix of songs: the Byrds, the Flying Burrito Brothers, obscure late-sixties Willie Nelson tracks. It was if I had encountered her in her own home, in her own life.

Startled by the unlikelihood of hearing this music in this place, I asked her about it—bypassing the usual strained talk about the weather and work—and our conversation led her eventually to reveal that she was, herself, a singer and songwriter and was moving soon to Nashville to try her luck in the industry. In fact, she had brought her mandolin with her to work and would be happy to play something for me that she had written. My haircut finished, she lifted the plastic protective cape from me and shook it, then slipped into the back room, returned with her instrument, tuned up, and began to play—as I sat, an audience of one, in my barber's chair. She was good, astonishingly so: her voice supple and full of feeling, her lyrics smart and evocative, her mandolin picking swift and precise. When she finished, I applauded, wished her luck, and added ten dollars to the tip.

By having found true music—spontaneous, personal—where I least expected it, I had been jolted out of complacency, shocked into joy.

Decades ago, supermarkets played for their customers placid, anodyne instrumental versions of middle-of-the-road pop hits: "Love Is a Many Splendored Thing," maybe, or "What the World Needs Now." Then the music got hipper: stores began to play original recordings of old hits or even almost hits. Pushing my cart down the dairy aisle, I have been surprised to be accompanied by "Day After Day" by Badfinger. A couple of songs later, Steely Dan's "Bad Sneakers" appears, and there is euphoria among the cornflakes. Grocery shopping is a mindless chore, but hearing such songs makes me feel rewarded for being there.

Once, in the store of a giant national chain, my mind on little but my search for chunky peanut butter, I flinched at the sudden rifle shot of loud drums accompanied by churning guitars, and then the discordant voice of Axl Rose, like jagged fingernails dragged across the surface of my brain. It was "Welcome to the Jungle"—ugly, belligerent, as if it wanted me out of the store immediately. I hurried to finish my shopping.

What corporate employee had added this song to the playlist, as if intent on antagonizing shoppers not just with the sound of the music but with the lyrics, a maniacal take on the language of retail culture: "We are the people that can find whatever you need. / If you got the money, honey, we got your disease"? Whoever that employee was, I have to hand it to him: the song startled me awake from a daydream. By seeming itself not to belong, it alerted me to where I was and to how at ease I felt being that dangerous thing: an unthinking, contented consumer, humming along half-consciously while I scanned the shelves.

It is one thing to see a favorite artist in concert: to willfully seek a powerful experience of music you care about. It is another, and maybe more profound, thing to stumble unexpectedly in a public space onto music that rouses and disorients you, breaking your routine, necessitating a recalibration of your relationship to reality. Once, on a family car trip of several days and hundreds of miles of unchanging interstate, we exited the highway to fill the tank. Across the street from the gas station, across a broad field of grass, was a band shell, and a hundred or so people sat before it in the dusk in folding chairs. Curious, we parked and locked the car, and my wife and two sons, one and three years old, walked toward the crowd. Music was playing—a small orchestra of woodwinds and brass. At a discreet distance, we sat on the grass, leaned back, and listened. Instrumental versions of standards—Irving Berlin, Cole Porter, George Gershwin—wafted toward us. This was a community band, not bad at all, playing a free summer show for the locals, who applauded warmly.

We did not know these people or the name of the town they lived in; we knew only that we were somewhere, anywhere, in Upstate New York and had pulled over for gas, intent on putting a hundred more miles on the odometer before we slept that night. But we found music, and we did not want to leave it just yet. As we listened, I felt my mind clearing of images of the highway and of my mission to get us to where we were going, which no longer mattered as much as this did. We lingered for more songs, even as shadows lengthened and vanished in the dusk, even as we grew pleasingly sleepy, our toddlers dancing in the grass.

33 | *Listening in a Crowd*

One sparkling sunny day in the late eighties, my first wife and I, on a whim, drove to Chapel Hill, North Carolina, a hundred miles from our home, to see what we could see. Strolling through nearby Carrboro, we passed the marquee of a music club and couldn't believe our luck: one of our favorite musicians, John Prine, was performing that night, and tickets were still available. We sprung for two, spent a few hours wandering Chapel Hill, then arrived early to the show. We were lucky again: we found two seats up front, inches from the small stage, on the edge of which I placed my beer. A few songs into the show, with Prine only feet from me, so close that with a false move he might topple my drink, he began to strum and pick a melody I recognized. Could it be? Could my luck go this far? He was playing a relatively obscure song of his but one of my favorites, a tune that could bring me near to weeping: "One Red Rose." This was my song; I'd sung it in my head so often that, as far as I was concerned, I was the character in it. From my own life, I recognized the lyrics' details: in a house gone dark and still, lying beneath the covers with my curly-haired love, listening to rain patter on a tin roof, talking softly, and then—the relationship over—being left with only the aching memory of such moments, astonished that any of them had happened. The song's sadness had long since become my sadness, its wonder my wonder. As I watched Prine sing the words I knew so well, a slight metaphysical bewilderment arose in me. *He* knew my song, too?

Of course I understood that the tune had been born from his own imagination; he had written and recorded it, and tens of thousands of other fans had probably listened to it with pleasure. But my experience of the song was mine alone, an entirely private one, an ongoing relationship in my mind between me and the recording Prine had completed years before, as if the more I listened to the song and played it back in my head, the more it came to seem made solely of my own thoughts. To be hearing it live now, performed by the songwriter himself, felt a little wrong, as if, note by note, he were taking the song back from me.

Attending a concert of a musician we admire, we make room for others—the musician, of course, but also all of the like-minded who have gathered with us. There is comfort in that: we recognize that we are part of a tribe; although we are strangers to one another, we share an understanding about at least this one thing. How unsettling it is, though, to be listening to a performance of a song that matters to you, that has helped you live your life, that you have carried for years in your secret heart, that you have sung in solitude to offer yourself solace, and to hear the woman two seats to the right of you singing along, getting every word exactly right, and then to glance at her and see that her eyes are welling with tears. It is her song, too. You're not sure whether to feel heartened or appalled.

I attended my first popular music concert when I was ten; it was a birthday present. Donovan, only twenty-three but already a little past the height of his fame, came to Seattle to sit alone, cross-legged on a rug, on a big stage in a cavernous downtown arena. Washing outward from the stage was a sea of people, mainly in their teens and twenties, some of them sitting, some of them standing, on the floor that the next night, when the hockey team was in town, would be covered with ice. In my seat a few rows up from the floor, I watched those people as often as I watched Donovan—the way two of them would leap to their feet to dance, then a few more would follow their example, then they would one by one, energy or interest flagging, sit down again; the way one of them would wave her hand furiously in the direction of a friend, far across the floor, who would return the wave; the way a large, green balloon suddenly appeared, bounding lazily above the crowd, as one person after another took a turn swatting it upward. These people were vivid individuals but also a single, fluidly moving social organism; the event seemed as much about them as about Donovan.

Ever since, I have surprised myself at almost every concert by having forgotten that the event is not about musicians performing for me; it is about musicians performing for *us*—including those as interested in swatting a balloon as in listening to music; and those who are gossiping gleefully about their incompetent boss and who, when Van Morrison closes his eyes to whisper-sing of the divinely illuminated face of his love, must raise their voices so as to be heard above him; and those who keep their phones glowing in the dark as Norah Jones performs so that, throughout the evening, they might twist in their seat, snap another photo of themselves with the singer as backdrop, and post it to Instagram with the caption "Guess where I am!"; and those who, half-drunk to begin with, obliviously jostle the bodies of strangers next to them, becoming wholly attentive to what Bob Dylan is doing only when he sings, "Everybody must get stoned," at which point they raise their Bud Lights in salute and let loose sodden yowls of agreement.

Before recorded music, this is the only way people listened to songs: communally, whether in a small group in the family parlor or in an audience of a thousand in a grand concert hall, amid whatever sneezing and jeering and whistling and elbowing and rising to rush to the bathroom that comes when other humans are around. Records, tapes, and CDs have spoiled and misled me, allowing me such solitary, intimate, intense experiences of listening that, when I attend a concert, I have to remind myself all over again that whatever pleasure I might experience will be of a different and probably more superficial order. It might have as much to do with the mild satisfactions of feeling part of a community of listeners, of bonding with them in a social ritual, as with hearing whatever is coming from the stage. My imagination, hungry to interact, unimpeded, with music, might not get its fill.

On one night of concert-going—only one—it has been otherwise. In the 1990s, my sister and I had seen Graham Parker, one of our favorite musicians, a couple of times at a cramped club in Washington, D.C. However, we had never found good seats there; in fact, the club didn't have many seats—most of the crowd stood—so our thrill at seeing and hearing Parker had been tempered by our gazing at the backs of heads in front of us and hearing drink orders hollered out at the bar behind us. There were, we surmised, perhaps two completely satisfactory seats in the whole place: at a table in the balcony, house right, overlooking the stage. After standing in long lines to enter the club and then watching those ahead of us stride swiftly to the best spots in the venue, we vowed that, the next time Parker came to town, we would arrive much earlier.

We did—so early that we were the only ones there, standing outside the closed door in the rain. We wondered if we might slip inside. We tried the door—it was unlocked. Inside, we stood for a couple of minutes, seeing no one but suspecting that an employee would soon shoo us outside. Then from across the small lobby a man walked toward us, a diminutive, thin fellow with a receding hairline. "How you doin'?" he said, in a British accent. "Mind if I play pinball?" It was Graham Parker. "It calms my nerves before a show."

For the next few minutes, we watched Parker play pinball, I leaning against a wall at a discreet distance, Dana being giddy and courageous enough to stand nearer, just to the side of the machine, and engage him in the smallest of small talk. We both felt too polite or dumbfounded to regale him with the story of our devotion to his music.

He ambled off, toward the inner regions of the club. When we heard, from within, drums and guitars bashing out a tune, we pushed our luck further and wandered upstairs, to the back balcony, near the mixing board. Parker and his band were onstage, doing a sound check. We stayed for the whole thing, several songs, feeling as though Parker were singing for only us. The music alone entered our ears, unaccompanied by the loud, random chatter of strangers or a "We love you, Graham!" or "'Free Bird'!" bellowed from the back of the crowd. No one had asked us to leave, and no one did. Untorn tickets still in our pockets, we made ourselves comfortable in the club's two best seats and didn't budge, watching as the rest of the customers filed in. The concert that followed was fun but unnecessary. Already, as if in a dream, we had attended a concert from which all other audience members had vanished. Already, as is the case with a dream, our imaginations were sated.

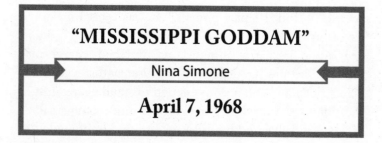

"MISSISSIPPI GODDAM"

Nina Simone

April 7, 1968

Some songs, nonetheless, are not wholly themselves unless a crowd is listening. The very fact of their being performed live—now, here, to the ears that need them—is the lightning that jolts them to life.

Nina Simone wrote her rollicking, enraged diatribe against racism, "Mississippi Goddam," in 1963, in response to the Birmingham church bombing that killed four young African-American girls. The song is a ferocious demand for equality in which Simone shows no patience for the theory that the achievement of full civil rights must be incremental, nor does she seem interested in engaging in a dialogue with her subjugators: "Don't tell me," she snarls, "I'll tell you."

The song is all about community: the community of the nation—especially several Southern states she accuses and curses by name—that has failed to live up to its promises; the community of African-Americans that the song, with its candid, unmannerly blast of condemnation, defends and emboldens; and the community of Black band members who perform the song, since it includes extended sections of call-and-response, in which the male musicians affirm Simone's complaints about American society's lack of progress with shouts of "Too slow!" It is difficult to imagine a studio recording of the song that could sizzle with electricity in the way a live performance does; it is no accident that "Mississippi Goddam" appeared first on a concert album.

Much of the song's power in any live performance is the sense of the audience absorbing and reacting to its startling honesty and lack of propriety. The tune is up-tempo, with the kind of zing familiar from songs of exuberant celebration. In her original 1964 concert recording, Simone jokes, "This is a show tune, but the show hasn't been written for it yet." In fact, the music's jauntiness does not feel far from the swooping gestures of the title song of *Oklahoma!*, but instead of Simone's melody rising toward a joyful assertion about the sweet prairie scent of wheat after rain, it rises toward a curse: "Mississippi goddam!"

On April 4, 1968, Martin Luther King, Jr., was assassinated in Memphis. Three days later, after some hesitation, Simone kept her date at the Westbury Music Fair on Long Island. When she performed "Mississippi Goddam," she sang it in a way, and in a context, that could not have occurred the week before and could never be replicated.

Her recorded performance is alternately furious and despondent, as if she is weary, after all these years, of having to argue her case, even while feeling a fresh necessity do so. Part of the tension of the performance is that, in the immediate wake of the killing of a Christian minister, Simone mourns him while saying publicly what he never would: she blasphemes, calling out, "Goddam!" and, while at first pleading for someone to "say a prayer," later admits, "I've even stopped believing in prayer." She adapts her lyrics to the occasion. Where she has otherwise sung, "Tennessee made me lose my rest," Simone now pointedly replaces "Tennessee" with the more specific "Memphis," the city of the assassination. At another point, instead of complaining about Tennessee, she updates the song by mentioning Lurleen Wallace, who had succeeded her segregationist husband as governor of Alabama and pursued his policies. This is less a show tune than a folk tune—an ever-elastic piece of music that lives in the air, in the moment of its being heard, and that changes according to the exigencies of the occasion. In its use as a form to report on the latest racial injustices, it prepares us for a work such as Claudia Rankine's book *Citizen*—a searing interrogation of racism in the twenty-first century, which was first published in 2014. The book includes a list of Black victims of racist killings, and with each reprinting of Rankine's book, the list changes: it gets longer.

The most powerful moment in Simone's post-assassination performance of the song comes during a spoken interlude that becomes a call to action—even a call to arms. She refers directly to King and to herself as part of a movement, and she implores her audience to become involved in it:

> Now you heard him. He's one of you. If you have been moved at *all*—and you know my songs at *all*—for God's sakes *join* me. Don't sit back there. The time is too late now. Good God. You know? The king is *dead*. The king of love is dead.

Then she startles her listeners, maybe even herself. Rejecting, half-kiddingly, King's famous methods of protest, she declares, with some threat and swagger, "I ain't 'bout to be nonviolent, honey!" In response, the crowd cheers and squeals delightedly, and, maybe in spite of herself, Simone laughs loudly, freely. She and her listeners are in this moment together, as art and determination hold their own against loss, a moment in which singer and audience alike are alive, attentive, seemingly ready for anything.

34 | *Secular Hymns*
—Music and the Metaphysical

What better way than music to describe the invisible?
—Dana Gioia

If some essential metaphysical truth, some fundamental order, underlies human existence, can a song make us sense it? The ancient Greeks thought so. Orpheus' music, said to embody sacred mysteries, was so much the song of the essence of being that it charmed animals, trees, stones, and rivers, which moved to its melodies, and it earned Orpheus temporary entrance, before his time, to the underworld. For centuries, the Western church has used music—Gregorian chants, hymns, the ebullient gospel of the Black church—to lift the faithful toward experience of the divine.

The lines between gospel music, rhythm and blues, and rock and roll were blurred from the start, with Little Richard, Sam Cooke, Aretha Franklin, Al Green, and any number of other singers moving fluidly from the choir to the concert stage. This seems no accident. Whether God is a distant promise from on high or is present only here and now, in the body, offering us no salvation beyond dancing, any urgent, rollicking tune—call it gospel or rock and roll—might wake us to his presence.

For Schopenhauer, unlike for many philosophers, music does not exist merely on the physical plane, evoking familiar human emotions and experiences. It has a metaphysical component; it gestures toward ultimate reality: the unifying force, beyond opposites and the dimensions of time and space, that motivates all of being. Music is not an escape *from* reality but an escape *into* a deeper reality, and the escape is accomplished—through stealth and indirection—entirely inside ourselves. In *The World as Will and Representation,* Schopenhauer writes, "[A] way *from within* stands open to us to that real inner nature of things to which we cannot penetrate *from without.* It is, so to speak, a subterranean passage, a secret alliance, which, as if by treachery, places us all at once in the fortress that could not be taken by attack from without."

Schopenhauer would likely be skeptical of the power of a modern pop song to reveal the "real inner nature of things," since, for him, words are a corrupting influence on music's ability to connect us to the metaphysical. He saw opera and any song with lyrics as inferior to wholly instrumental music, at least as a means of bringing us close to the fundamental nature of things, since that nature is beyond the categorizing, defining function of words. Once a piece of music becomes a dramatization of a particular, identifiable human reality, it shrinks and turns away from the ineffable force that unites all of human reality: "[music] never expresses the phenomenon, but only the inner nature, the in-itself, of every phenomenon, the will itself. Therefore music does not express this or that particular and definite pleasure, this or that affliction, pain, sorrow, horror, gaiety, merriment, or peace of mind, but joy, pain, sorrow, horror, gaiety, merriment, peace of mind *themselves,* to a certain extent in the abstract, their essential nature, without any accessories, and so also without the motives for them."

For Schopenhauer, the fact of our existing in a body is a means of approaching the transcendent, but it is also an impediment to fully arriving there. Because of our senses and imagination, music works upon us to suggest a larger, incompletely knowable order, yet even the most powerful music cannot melt the boundary between us and the ultimate. To cross that boundary would be to go beyond what our consciousness is capable of; it would mean to vanish, to no longer be a self. The paradox is the one Keats recognizes in "Ode to a Nightingale," written a year after Schopenhauer published his thoughts on music. The poet praises the bird whose song is a promise of escape from the travails of life. He yearns to meld with that song, beyond the world of human pain, but, knowing that the only means of such an escape is dying, he laments, "Still wouldst thou sing, and I have ears in vain."

A song might not deliver us completely to a transcendent reality, yet we need it to jostle us out of the numbing rhythms of dailiness, to give form to our wondering about what exists beyond the boundary of our knowing—about the ultimate structure that might underlie everything, whether that structure involves the glorious, eternally revivifying force of divine love, a vast blankness, or something in between. Proust's narrator describes his experience of hearing an especially moving piece of music as presenting him "the promise and proof that there existed something other, realisable no doubt by art, than the nullity that I had found in all my pleasures and in love itself, and that if my life seemed to me so empty, at least there were still regions unexplored."

Some songs serve for me as secular hymns, as honorings of such unexplored, maybe unexplorable, regions; listening to them, I feel the richness and mystery of my existing in the first place, a mystery that can be only sensed, never solved. Van Morrison's "Cleaning Windows" narrates a day of manual labor so abounding in sensory pleasures that they seem all that is necessary for a life of meaning. In the first verse alone, all five of the singer's senses are alert to the world: to the weight of the ladders he and his coworker carry down the street; to the wrought-iron gates they walk past; to the smell of a bakery wafting from across the road; to the sound of a Jimmie

Rodgers record; to the taste of Woodbine cigarettes. Later he presents a litany of the blues music he is listening to and books he is reading, and these pleasures seem inextricably bound up with the routines of his working life. The physical, repetitive labor of washing windows becomes a ritual that maintains the singer's focus on the sensory world in the present moment. When Morrison exults, "I'm happy cleaning windows," he might as well be saying he is happy being alive. The only holiness we need, the song tells me, is already here, in all kinds of random, fleeting quotidian delights, provided we are alert to them. As Morrison incants in another song, "It ain't why why why why why why why why why why why why why why why why why why why. It ain't why: it just is."

"Cleaning Windows" celebrates an idea Emerson proposed two centuries ago, that any of us can discover the heaven that is earthly existence if only we attend to the house—the immediate daily existence—that happens to be ours: "Know then, that the world exists for you . . . . All that Adam had, all that Caesar could, you have and can do. Adam called his house, heaven and earth; Caesar called his house, Rome; you perhaps call yours, a cobler's trade; a hundred acres of ploughed land; or a scholar's garret"—or, Emerson might have added, the ladder, rag, and bucket of the window cleaner.

Vic Chesnutt's "Myrtle," with its dreamily unhurried tempo and spare, plinking piano, leaves plenty of room, plenty of silent spaces, for mystery to dwell. When the singer senses something about existence bigger than he is, something he cannot "substantiate," I feel the horror, amazement, and necessity in his act of sacrificing almost everything, even the stability of his selfhood, to know that thing directly: "whittled with an X-Acto knife," he sings, "plumb right through my load-bearing wall."

While a song cannot name the thing it senses that is by definition beyond naming, it can make us feel that thing's presence—it can open us to this mystery it is haunted by. Paradoxically, to put us in mind of what transcends time, words, and music, the song makes use of time, words, and music. It carries us to the threshold between those things and their absence, between knowing and not knowing, between articulateness and wordlessness, to the edge of the metaphysical realm. "Music gives us ontological messages," philosopher William James says. "There is a verge of the mind which these things haunt; and whispers therefrom mingle with the operations of our understanding, even as the waters of the infinite ocean send their waves to break among the pebbles that lie upon our shores."

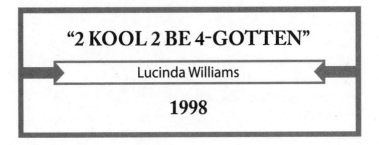

"2 KOOL 2 BE 4-GOTTEN"

Lucinda Williams

1998

The first words are a litany of negations—an erasure of preconceptions, an existential cleansing:

> You can't depend on anything really
> There's no promises, there's no point
> There's no good, there's no bad
> In this dirty little joint

The joint, we learn, is the Magic City juke joint in Rosedale, Mississippi, but, considering how many disparate bits of reality congregate there, it could be all the world. The song is a collage, many of its details taken from photographs by Birney Imes and Shelby Lee Adams, but the disconnected images cohere through the force of Williams' unbounded, egalitarian vision. One feels that, in this song, anything might be said, any object in the world might make an appearance, and it would fit, for the song's subject seems to be all of human existence itself, in its multiplicity and mystery. For us to truly experience that existence, the song's initial lines suggest, we must enter this juke joint without illusions, our imaginations freed from conventional, fixed measurements of meaning and morality. Without ponderously, self-consciously doing so—there is too much wonder, too much openness to surprise in the song for that—"2 Kool 2 Be 4-Gotten" becomes about nothing less than the problem of how to live, with integrity and urgency, a life that is certain to end and that offers only the barest of instructions.

The groove is laid-back, cool, the tempo relaxed, the singing restrained, close to mere talking, as if Williams' job is not to emote but to report, letting the facts of the juke joint speak for themselves. Those facts suggest that this place is not without order: "House rules, no exceptions," she announces, and other lines combine into something like a juke joint Ten Commandments:

> No dope smoking, no beer sold after twelve o'clock . . .
> No bad language, no gambling, no fighting
> Sorry, no credit, don't ask

Once one allows for the possibility that the song's setting represents an existential vision of reality, the line "Sorry, no credit, don't ask" seems less an arbitrarily chosen quote of a posted juke joint policy than the basis of a metaphysics. The self is alive only in this body, and in this moment, free of the burden of following some culturally imagined cosmic law yet burdened, in turn, by the weight of the moment and the consequences of individual choice. The life we have is ours alone.

"Sorry, no credit": we pay for our choices now, and continually, making no bargains with the present to avoid responsibility.

Further signaling that her setting is not just a typical juke joint, Williams informs us that someone long dead—someone famously rumored to have made his own fateful choice—is alive there. Robert Johnson "sings over in a corner by the bar. / Sold his soul to the devil so he can play guitar." Johnson's kind of decision is one means of living intensely and purposefully within the shadow of our own demise, and the ultimate consequence of such a choice is perhaps the only sure way we have of conquering that death: by remaining in the minds of those who live after us—by being unforgettable. "Too cool to be forgotten," Williams muses. Another option available to us is a Kierkegaardian leap of faith: on the joint's bathroom wall is the message "Is God the answer? Yes." A man "running through the grass outside" seems to have made such a leap and is intent on testing the power that he believes comes with it, claiming that he will "take up serpents" and "drink the deadly thing / And it will not hurt him."

If God is not the answer, perhaps earthly love is. In the final verse, the singer leaves the setting of the juke joint, seeming to have been nudged by its implications into contemplation of a personal memory. She once had a lover she thought would "always" be her "Valentine," but that sentimental neglect of the power of time was replaced with a stark realization of her aloneness within, and responsibility for, her own existence. When, at the railing of a bridge that crossed a Louisiana river, her lover asked her to jump with him, she understood that his end did not have to be hers: "I told him, 'No way, baby, that's your own death, you see.'"

Halfway through the song, and again near its conclusion, an enigmatic line appears: "June bug vs. Hurricane"—one of the phrases scrawled on the juke joint wall in a photo that Williams studied. She offers it in the song without explanation (it could refer to anything from prizefighters to cocktails), but it fits. The confrontation of June bug and Hurricane might be a version of the deathless tale of an underdog fighting a seemingly indomitable foe: Jacob and the angel, Job and his Lord, Ahab and Moby Dick, any one of us and the life that will annihilate us, given time. But before that happens, the song seems to say, we can take hold of the present moment with dignity and urgency, as if our lives matter, for if they don't, what does?

"HELLHOUND ON MY TRAIL"

Robert Johnson

1937

The blues poet has been where we are all afraid to go, as if there was a physical place, a forbidden place that corresponds to a place in ourselves where we experience the tragic sense of life and its amazing wonders. In that dive, in that all-night blues and soul club, we feel the full weight of our fate, we taste the nothingness at the heart of our being, we are simultaneously wretched and happy, we spit on it all, we want to weep and raise hell, because the blues, in the end, is about a sadness older than the world, and there's no cure for that.

— Charles Simic

As the record begins, there is little sign of trouble. Loping guitar chords meander downward, not unpleasantly; they are leading us somewhere but portend no evident menace or conflict. Then the singer enters, and all is changed—we are suddenly somewhere bleak and harrowing. The voice is tense, restless, high-pitched, a hint of a wail and shiver in it. It makes no sense that Johnson, when he made this recording, was only twenty-six; he sounds eighty or ninety or five hundred, an ageless figure calling out from within some ancient myth, perhaps from within Simic's "forbidden place," a figure shaking with dread and dark knowledge.

The first thing he tells us is that he must "keep moving," but what he is fleeing seems as much inside him as outside. "Blues falling down like hail," he proclaims, the weather entering the song only as the vehicle in a simile, instructing us that, however much we might visualize the character traveling through a physical landscape, the world he moves through is first of all emotional and psychological; it is the realm within him of relentless blues, a realm he cannot escape, in which— with a hound unleashed from hell intent on dragging him under—existence has been distilled to a single imperative: to not sit still. The singer seems damned already; the song offers no hope of conventional religious salvation. We might think of him as the Robert Johnson referred to in the Lucinda Williams tune: the poor country boy who met the devil at the crossroads and traded his soul for otherworldly skill on guitar. But "Hellhound on My Trail" feels bigger than that, its plot too wayward and wide, its mood too grim and all consuming, not to render as irrelevant any reading of the song as a tidy drama of cause and effect. It feels, instead, like an entire world, maybe the world within this one, an existence pared down to the rudiments of human desire and disquiet.

The metaphysical plane that the song inhabits is constricted and shadowy, the setting reduced to austere particulars of time and weather, amid which there is no possibility of grace, only the immediate consequences of a false move or a lucky one. What matters is how long the singer can outrun the hound and whether, in the meantime, such a life can afford him any pleasure.

If no spiritual salvation is possible, at least temporary physical gratification might be: not divine love but earthly love. In the second verse, there is something surprising, even subversive, in the singer's reference to Christmas. "If today was Christmas Eve / And tomorrow was Christmas Day," he sings, plucking the guitar strings forcefully, discordantly, so they seem to wail, and then he follows those lines by referring not to any spiritual sustenance the holiday might bring but to sexual pleasure. Suddenly introducing into the song the character of a lover, his "little sweet rider," he says more than sings, in a way that seems half come-on, half happy daydream, "Aww, wouldn't we have a time, baby?" The only possible salvation available to him—maybe the only one he yearns for—is one that is bound to the corporeal and temporal world: the earthly transcendence of sensual pleasure that, as Johnson sings, can help him "pass the time away."

But the character seems destined to obey his "ramblin' mind." There seems no place he can stay put, no occasion that does not hint at the menace that haunts him. His fate is augured in everything: in the rising wind, in "the leaves tremblin' on the tree," and even in the guitar string that—as he sings of those leaves—cries out twice, as if frightened itself.

He ends the song by claiming, "All I need's my little sweet woman / To keep my company," but he might be whistling past the graveyard—or past the gates of hell. His belief that all he needs is his woman feels genuine, but what power could that faith wield against the metaphysical weather that surrounds him? The song seems to have no answer. Throughout the recording, Johnson's voice is filled with unease, and his playing with frenzy and agitation, as if the guitar would leap from his grasp, abandoning him to meet his fate alone—a fate no earthly love, of woman or of music, has magic enough to conquer.

35 | *To the Edge of Ecstasy*

Some songs are dangerous, at least for those wary of los-ing control. When a singer gives in to the music—to its rhythms and incantations—and to the lyrics' mysterious, unspoken implications, she can follow the song past her own understanding, past the comforting sense that the world is orderly and knowable, back into the wordless and elemental, from which the music comes, maybe from which she herself comes. A trusting listener can follow her there.

Van Morrison's "And the Healing Has Begun" begins with four minutes of joyful prophesying, four minutes of Morrison repeatedly proclaiming that he and his lover will one day begin to heal and will stride down the avenue sing-ing all of the old songs, four minutes of Toni Marcus' violin winding around, beneath, and above the singer's insistent pronouncements, then taking the song itself by force, as if transforming Morrison's vision into pure music, answering his assertions with a wordless confirmation of their truth, lifting the song out of time. Then Morrison, as if carried off by the music into that imagined future of renewal and wholeness, yelps, "Ow!—I can't stand myself!"

We might call this ecstasy. The word comes from the an-cient Greek *ekstasis*, meaning to *stand outside* oneself, which, in its suggestion of passing through a boundary, implies a loss of control, of will, of ego: the self exists but without a sense of its separateness and without, therefore, the volition that comes with belief in such separateness.

In his conception of the ideal, orderly state, Plato banished music that would lead to such derangement. Aristotle, too, was distrustful of music that was central to Dionysian rituals and that, as the British psychiatrist Anthony Storr wrote, was based "upon the idea that individuals could be purged of irrational impulses or cured of madness if they temporarily lost all inhibitions and 'let go' in an ecstatic fashion." For Aristotle, such music was "too orgiastic and emotional."

Orgiastic and emotional: that is exactly what much popular music aims to be. When Little Richard lets out a falsetto shriek with a growl at its center, when Donna Summer moans and gasps her way through the pulsating rhythms of "Love to Love You Baby," when Johnny Rotten takes on the subject of abortion by bellowing, "I'm not an animal!" again and again, the abandoning of inhibitions seems the whole point.

But if to be ecstatic means to stand outside the self, then ecstasy involves something beyond merely the full, unchecked expression of deep feeling. It involves something like the opposite: a transcendence of feeling, an encroachment upon that which is beyond the self's private concerns, whether that thing be defined as divine light or chaotic darkness. For Nietzsche, one of the necessary forces in art is "Dionysian emotions," about which he wrote, "[A]s they grow in intensity everything subjective vanishes into complete self-forgetfulness." In such ecstasy, the self experiences "mystical self-abnegation."

Perhaps pure ecstasy, then, is beyond music's capacity to express, for if the self is obliterated, how can it be called upon to communicate its condition? Maybe the best that a song can do is journey to the edge of ecstasy, to the border between the self and its absence. Signs that a song has traveled to such a realm include the singer straying from the song's initial structure, as he begins to experience a condition he could not have anticipated when the singing began, and, as that condition overwhelms him, the language breaking down, becoming fragmented, discontinuous, even wordless—or surprising us, and the singer, with sudden explosions of awareness. The singer surrenders to his feeling, and that feeling moves him, as if in an act of inexplicable grace, past feeling, past the self, toward the overwhelming and unutterable.

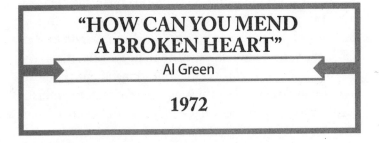

"HOW CAN YOU MEND A BROKEN HEART"

Al Green

1972

The song begins with delicate steadiness: the simple, metronomic drumbeats on the high hat and snare, the unadorned, circular guitar figure, the sustained organ chords that—although this is ostensibly a secular love song—give the arrangement a whiff of the church. For a few bars, wistful strings slip in, then discreetly vanish, as if careful not to say too much. Then Al Green, seeming in the same mood as the instrumentation, pensive and circumspect, begins to sing. "I can think of younger days," he muses, whispering nearly, as if aware that he has feelings worth singing about but wary of giving in to them fully. He floats along on the melody, landing lightly on the notes, clipping syllables. When he sings, "I was never told about the sorrow"—a line that another singer might bellow, selling his sadness to the cheap seats—Green understates the claim, as if the fact has only just now occurred to him, the word "sorrow" coming out of him almost as quiet as breathing.

The tone of the succeeding chorus is, if anything, even more subdued than that of the verse. Green sings the first of the chorus' list of questions, "And how can you mend a broken heart?" so airily that it is hardly there at all. The strings enter again, their plaintive sweetness seeming to urge the singer further into a reckoning with his despair. In the next line, his restraint begins to weaken; there is the slightest lift in volume, and a mild choke and tremble, in a few syllables: "How can you stop the *rain* from *falling down*?" With the next words—the imperative "Tell me"—the song begins to intimate that, for this singer, the chorus' litany of unanswerable questions about the heart and rain and turning world is not merely rhetorical. He is begging to understand what cannot be understood, and, at this vulnerable moment of private pain, Green finds himself suddenly not alone: female background singers enter, emboldening him, pleading along with him, "How can you stop the sun from shining?" They will stay with him until the song's end, accompanying him toward a place that he may yet have little sense of; he has only just begun his journey.

As the first chorus continues, the feeling deepens, with Green extending syllables, adding a little grit to his timbre, interjecting a muted affirmation—"yeah"—and, with the words "somebody *please*," leaping suddenly into a brief falsetto squeal. In the second verse, Green sings of feeling the breeze, and the strings answer him with a swirling figure, unsubtly mimicking the wind. The literalness of the sound, and its self-conscious, premeditated quality, places it just this side of cheesy. It is the last moment when the song will sound so in control of itself; from here, it will travel to parts unknown.

By the time Green returns to the chorus, he has begun to use the lyric not as an end but as a starting point, a pattern of verbal markers he slaloms around as he seeks out, and testifies to, the true nature of his pain. He annotates the lines with interjections: after referring to "a broken heart," he adds, "And *mine* is . . . ." While the background singers ask, smoothly and coherently, "How can you stop the sun from shining?" Green's own vocal fragments and only partially collects itself, as—omitting the "How" that begins his question—he sings, "Can you stop the s . . . —that old sun—from shining." He has found openings in the song for his feelings to slip through, feelings he might initially have been wary of conveying or even not fully aware of until the song made them rise from within him. In his singing now we hear the frenzy beneath the heartbreak, the impoverishment beneath the melancholy. But those are my own insufficient labels for what he feels, insufficient because his condition is ineffable. The lyric might name his problem as a "broken heart," but that cliché—a metaphor so familiar it cannot make us feel whatever strange, surprising rightness it might have had originally—obscures as much as clarifies the plight of the singer. No words can account completely for what he feels, as he admits implicitly when he sings, "And sometimes I have to say, yeah, say, / La-la-la / La-la-la."

When Green returns to expressing himself in words, he has journeyed to a place deep within the song, and within himself, that the first bars of this recording could not have foreshadowed. Instead of merely explaining that he needs someone, or something, to let him "live again," he is overwhelmed by that need; he sings from deep within it, testifying, preaching, in an urgent incantation, "I just wanna, I just wanna, I just wanna, I just wanna, I just wanna *live* again, baby." He extends the single syllable of "live" to three syllables that lift in pitch, like Lazarus rising from the tomb.

For the rest of the song, Green remains on that elevated plane, a kind of rapturous sadness, at one point serving witness to how his entire being—mind, soul, body, all that he is, all that he is capable of—is devoted to this urge to transcend the spiritual death he is suffering: "I *think* I, I *know* I, I *believe* I, I *feel* like I got to, I feel like I wanna *live* again!"

If he has not yet transcended his pain, he has transcended the written song—the text that he has, as it were, taken as inspiration for his extemporaneous testimony. When he sings, one final time, "How can you stop the rain from falling down?" the image is no longer a familiar, banal metaphor for melancholy. It is real; it is literal. Green shouts, "My clothes are all *wet!*" Through whatever force is at the center of his genius—some special power of imagination? of access to authentic feeling?—he makes the rain burst the bonds of the figurative. Suddenly there is a real downpour in this song, and the singer is drenched by it, fully immersed, as in a baptism. In a single shout, of anguish or joy or both, Green melds the experience of suffering with the promise of transcending it.

"How Can You Mend a Broken Heart," written and performed by the Bee Gees, was a worldwide hit in the summer of 1971, just a few months before Green recorded his version. As an eleven-year-old, I liked the Bee Gees record. I was pleased when it was played on the radio. When I hear it now, I enjoy the comforting way it returns me to that early, more innocent time in my life when I first came to know the record, to memorize its words and sing along with them. Whenever I listen to Al Green's cover of the tune, I do not—I cannot—sing along. I feel myself entirely in the present, slightly disoriented, uncertain what will happen next, as the song proceeds, deepens, and discovers itself. It remains, till the end, beyond my full comprehension; my imagination and intellect have no dominion over it. As the record fades, I feel not only that Al Green has been baptized by the song but that he has baptized it, remaking a simple, familiar tune into something complicatedly, mysteriously alive. And, with it, he has baptized me, too.

36 | *A Mind Full of Music,*
Reprise

My mind is full of music. I suspect that, in this way, I am like most people. The sounds seem intent on staying there. Elliott Smith is in me, offering to his lover the chilling explanation that he has no explanation, that he was "bad news" for her "just because." The opposite is in me, too—the joyful, surging monster pop of NRBQ's "I Want You Bad"—as is the beginning of Elvis Costello's "B Movie": its few swift measures of a jittery bass line that, for forty years, when I am thinking of nothing in particular, has risen to the surface of my consciousness, so I am humming it and hardly aware of doing so, as if those hurtling notes are my brain's default setting.

I seem to need these songs, but why them particularly? Who knows? Any song, no matter how paraphrasable its literal subject, is always about other things impossible to define precisely: feelings, states of being, buried memories, rhythms of thinking that the music—being wordless—can only gesture toward, not name. The songs are not merely messages; they are living, mysterious, dynamic entities that cannot exhaust themselves of energy and implication. They intensify my sense of being here—of existing as a single, distinctive person; they remind me that I am alive. And who is that "I"? If the self that I am is shifting, contingent, and always partially inscrutable, I nonetheless guess that the swirl of songs in my head, my private assemblage of sounds that won't let me forget them, is singing the song of who that self is.

The big, cantering drumbeat of "Cathy's Clown" by the Everly Brothers is in me, and "O-o-h Child" by the Five Stairsteps, bursting forth faithfully again and again like noon sun through the clouds, and even the Beatles' humble ditty "Her Majesty," less than half a minute long and incomplete, slightly. The track, the last one on *Abbey Road*, ends on an offbeat; the following downbeat is missing; the song does not resolve. I am charmed by the fact that the final song on the final album the Beatles recorded does not quite end, as if the Beatles themselves did not quite end, declining to finish their work. That last, absent note hangs in my mind, perfect and unheard. For most of my life, I have been waiting to hear it, grateful that I never will.

Acknowledgments

Writing this book—contemplating connections between songs and the self, and in doing so happily revisiting, with vigorous attention, songs that have mattered to me—has been a cause of constant joy. I am thankful to several people who, in one way or another, helped me keep that joy going, offering me experiences, advice, or encouragement as I journeyed from having an initial inkling of a subject worth pursuing toward completing the book: Nick Johnson, Gail Lewis, Jeffrey Gillespie, Mark Halliday, Gregory Orr, Matty Gervais, Charity Rose Thielen, Mikey Gervais, Chris Mercer, and Alessandra Lynch. I am grateful to my two sons, Milo and Oliver (aka Shy), who, as they began discovering music in their own lives, could not have known that I was watching and listening carefully, taking notes for my own secret purposes.

I also thank Butler University and the Arts Council of Indianapolis for the gift of time and funding that allowed me to finish this project. Gratitude as well to the students of Butler for their willingness to share with me their own experiences of music.

Deep thanks to Des Hewson, for the numerous insightful and elegant editing suggestions.

I am forever indebted to Pat McDonald, Rachel Bell, and the whole gang at Overcup Press for believing in and nurturing this eccentric little project.

Notes

Chapter 2

3 Neurological studies . . . : Levitin, p. 154.

4 "I do not know which to prefer": Stevens, p. 93.

4 "half create": Wordsworth, "Lines Composed . . . ," p. 110.

4 "the inrushing floodlight": Copland, p. 8.

5 Maybe that is because music integrates . . . : Levitin, pp. 85-6.

5 "moods and memories": Sacks, p. 385.

5 "Even if playing music were forbidden": Storr, p. 107.

6 "blessed rage for order": Stevens, p. 130.

6 "an increase of life, a sort of competition": Bachelard, p. xxix.

6 "Without music, life would be an error": Nietzsche, *The Portable Nietzsche*, p. 471.

Chapter 3

10 "musical works themselves serve as a prototype": Gracyk, p. 189-90.

11 "Because the song never plays the same way twice": Marcus, p. 98.

Chapter 7

29 "can see heroes and shipwrecks in the music's flood": Forster, p. 23.

29 "Now comes the wonderful movement": Forster pp. 24-5.

31 "At the peak, in 1980 or 1981": Lethem, p. 139.

35 "Pizzicato strings": *Speed Racer.*

Chapter 8
40 Billy Joel and James Taylor . . . : Van Campen, p. 92;
    Zollo, p. 522.
40 Stravinsky claimed . . . : Storr, p. 182.
41 "someone": Bede, p. 17.

Chapter 9
44 "Where does music enter?": "John Darnielle—*The Interview Show.*"
44 "One theory": Storr, p. 8.
44 Researchers have discovered . . . : Gracyk, p. 178.

Chapter 11
53 "become enraptured with the inescapable": Adorno,
    "On Popular Music," p. 447.
53 "is almost the same thing as to recognize it": Adorno,
    "On the Fetish Character," p. 288.
57 "If he listens to the radio every Saturday": Sartre,
    pp. 650-51.
57 "is on the chart because it's popular": quoted in Hajdu,
    Love for Sale, p. 73.

Chapter 12
64 "with a certain extension of trust": Willis, p. 49.

Chapter 13
67 "I am so beautiful": Collins, p. 80.

Chapter 14
76 "most people have formed their tastes": Levitin, p. 233.
78 "Oh god": Shaughnessy, p. 62.
79 "no amount of irony will ever quite": Halliday, "Ode:
    The Capris," p. 24.

Chapter 15

83 "our sense of identity and difference is established":
Frith, p. 18.

83 "Our group listens to this kind of music": Levitin,
p. 232.

86 "more dangerous enemies of truth than lies": Nietzsche,
The Portable Nietzsche, p. 63.

86 "the struggle between the instinct and the intellect":
Hepworth, p. 156.

87 "That was a really good record!": Willman.

Chapter 18

99 "The past is never dead": Faulkner, p. 73.

100 "It had immediately proposed to him particular
sensual pleasures": Proust, *Swann's Way*, pp. 217-18.

101 "And before Swann had time to understand": Proust,
Swann's Way, p. 358.

Chapter 19

103 "Who reaches for a book when your heart shatters":
Sound Opinions.

108 "engender empathy, not a standing ovation": Feinstein,
p. 69.

Chapter 20

112 "not about *dispelling* mystery": quoted in Zollo,
p. 631.

112 "Not the fruit of experience, but experience itself":
Pater, p. 188.

112 "mere intelligence": Pater, p. 108.

112 "All art": Pater, p. 106.

Chapter 21
121 "Time is always new": quoted in Sacks, footnote, p. 227.
121 "Rhythm is a form cut into TIME": Pound, p. 198.
122 "[I]f 'the present' is actually defined": Frith, p. 151.
122 "When everything is perfectly in time": quoted in Belluck.
123 "[W]hen hearing a phrase or a melody for the second time": quoted in Boruch, p. 166.

Chapter 22
130 "hand is ever at his lips / Bidding adieu": Keats, "Ode on Melancholy," p. 195.
131 "Holly's distinctive style lay mainly in": Willis, p. 44.

Chapter 24
146 "People who look for symbolic meanings": quoted in Perloff, p. 44.
147 "stand the standard distance / Distant strangers stand apart": Purple Mountains, "That's Just the Way That I Feel" and "Maybe I'm the Only One for Me."
150 "But the quartet practicing in the park": "'American Pie' Meaning."
150 "The words mustn't be precious or condescending": Furia, p. 176.

Chapter 25
158 "pop songs open the doors to dream": Hennion, p. 205.
158 "one cannot end a dream, 'full-stop,' just like that": Hennion, p. 191.

Chapter 28
173 "Building in any successful rock 'n' roll record":
     quoted in Frith, p. 158.

Chapter 29
176 "like smoke": Maher, p. 147.
176 "The frequent use of the direct style": Hennion, p. 197.
177 "[F]or the first time Swann's thoughts turned with a
     stab": Proust, *Swann's Way*, p. 361.
177 "Vinteuil had been dead for many years": Proust,
     Remembrance of Things Past, vol. 2, p. 557.

Chapter 32
202 "When I wasn't internally grumbling": Strayed, p. 85.

Chapter 34
217 "What better way than music to describe the
     invisible?": Tate, p. 215.
218 "[A] way *from within* stands open to us":
     Schopenhauer, vol. II, p. 195.
218 "[music] never expresses the phenomenon, but only
     the inner nature": Schopenhauer, vol. I, p. 261.
219 "Still wouldst thou sing": Keats, "Ode to a
     Nightingale," p. 184.
219 "the promise and proof that there existed something
     other": Proust, *Remembrance of Things Past*, vol. 2, p.
     563.
220 "Know then, that the world exists for you": Emerson,
     Nature, p. 48.
221 "Music gives us ontological messages": James, p. 421.
224 "The blues poet has been where we are all afraid to
     go": Simic, p. 52.

Chapter 35

228 "upon the idea that individuals could be purged":
Storr, p. 43.

228 "Dionysian emotions": Nietzsche, *The Birth of Tragedy*,
p. 38.

Bibliography

Adorno, Theodor. "On the Fetish Character in Music and the Regression of Listening." *Essays on Music*, edited by Richard Leppert and translated by Susan H. Gillespie, UCalifornia, 2002, pp. 288-317.

---. "On Popular Music." *Essays on Music*, edited by Richard Leppert and translated by Susan H. Gillespie, UCalifornia, 2002, pp. 437-469.

"'American Pie' Meaning." CBS News, 29 March 2017, https://www. cbsnews.com/news/don-mclean-explains-why-he-wont-reveal-the-meaning-of-american-pie/?intcid=CNM-00-10abd1h.

Bachelard, Gaston. *The Poetics of Space*. Translated by Maria Jolas, Beacon, 1969.

Bede. "The Story of Cædmon." *The Norton Anthology of English Literature*, 6th edition, edited by M. H. Abrams, et al., vol. 1, Norton, 1993, pp. 17-19.

Belluck, Pam. "To Tug Hearts, Music First Must Tickle the Neurons." *New York Times*, 18 April 2011, https://www.nytimes. com/2011/04/19/science/19brain.html.

Boruch, Marianne. "Poetry's Over and Over." *In the Blue Pharmacy*. Trinity UP, 2005, pp. 164-182.

Collins, Billy. "Nightclub." *Sailing Alone Around the Room: New and Selected Poems*. Random House, 2001, pp. 80-1.

Copland, Aaron. *Music and Imagination*. Harvard UP, 1952.

Emerson, Ralph Waldo. *Nature. Emerson: Essays and Lectures*, edited by Joel Porte, Library of America, 1983, pp. 5-49.

Faulkner, William. *Requiem for a Nun*. Vintage, 1994.

Feinstein, Michael, with Ian Jackman. *The Gershwins and Me: A Personal History in Twelve Songs*. Simon and Schuster, 2012.

Forster, E. M. *Howards End*. Bantam, 1985.

Frith, Simon. *Performing Rights: On the Value of Popular Music.* Harvard UP, 1996.

Furia, Philip. *Ira Gershwin: The Art of the Lyricist.* Oxford UP, 1997.

Gracyk, Theodore. *Listening to Popular Music: Or, How I Learned to Stop Worrying and Love Led Zeppelin.* UMichigan Press, 2007.

Hajdu, David. *Love for Sale: Pop Music in America.* Farrar, Straus and Giroux, 2016

Halliday, Mark. "Ode: The Capris." *Tasker Street.* UMassachusetts, 1992, pp. 23-4.

---. "The Schuylkill." *Jab.* UChicago, 2002, p. 55.

Hennion, Antoine. "The Production of Success: An Antimusicology of the Pop Song." *On Record: Rock, Pop, and the Written Word,* edited by Simon Frith & Andrew Goodwin, Routledge, 1990, pp. 185-206

Hepworth, David. *Never a Dull Moment: 1971—The Year That Rock Exploded.* Henry Holt, 2016.

James, William. *The Varieties of Religious Experience: A Study in Human Nature.* Penguin, 1982.

"John Darnielle—The Interview Show." PBS, uploaded 21 Feb. 2019, www.pbs.org/video/john-darnielle-interview-show-3egniq.

Keats, John. "Ode on Melancholy." *The Complete Poems of John Keats.* Modern Library, 1994, pp. 194-5.

---. "Ode to a Nightingale." *The Complete Poems of John Keats.* Modern Library, 1994, pp. 183-5.

Lethem, Jonathan. *The Disappointment Artist: Essays.* Knopf/ Doubleday, 2007.

Levitin, Daniel J. *This Is Your Brain on Music: The Science of a Human Obsession.* Dutton, 2016.

Maher, Paul, Jr., editor. *Tom Waits on Tom Waits: Interviews and Encounters.* Aurum, 2001.

Marcus, Greil. *Like a Rolling Stone: Bob Dylan at the Crossroads.* Public Affairs, 2005.

Nietzsche, Friedrich. *The Birth of Tragedy.* Translated by Walter Kaufmann, Random House, 1967.

---. *The Portable Nietzsche*. Edited and translated by Walter Kaufmann, Penguin, 1976.

Pater, Walter. *The Renaissance: Studies in Art and Poetry*, edited by Donald L. Hill, U California Press, 1980.

Perloff, Marjorie. *The Poetics of Indeterminacy: Rimbaud to Cage*. Northwestern UP, 1999.

Pound, Ezra. "Treatise on Metre." *ABC of Reading*. New Directions, 1960, pp. 195-206.

Proust, Marcel. *Remembrance of Things Past*. Translated by C.K. Scott Moncrieff, vol. 2, Random House, 1932.

---. *Swann's Way*. Translated by Lydia Davis, Penguin, 2004.

Purple Mountains. *Purple Mountains*, Drag City, 2019.

Sacks, Oliver. *Musicophilia: Tales of Music and the Brain*. Vintage, 2008.

Sartre, Jean-Paul. *Critique of Dialectical Reason*, Vol. I. Translated by Alan Sheridan-Smith, Verso, 2002.

Schopenhauer, Arthur. *The World as Will and Representation*. Translated by E. F. J. Payne, Dover, 1966. 2 vols.

Shaughnessy, Brenda. *So Much Synth*. Copper Canyon, 2016.

Simic, Charles. *The Unemployed Fortune-Teller: Essays and Memoirs*. UMichigan, 1994.

Sound Opinions podcast #716, WBEZ, 16 August 2019. WBEZ, https://www.soundopinions.org/show/716.

Speed Racer: Welcome to the World of Vic Chesnutt. Directed by Peter Sillen, 1994.

Stevens, Wallace. *The Collected Poems of Wallace Stevens*. Knopf, 1993.

Storr, Anthony. *Music and the Mind*. The Free Press, 1992.

Strayed, Cheryl. *Wild*. Vintage, 2013.

Tate, James, editor. *The Best American Poetry 1997*. Simon & Schuster, 1997.

Van Campen, Cretien. *The Proust Effect: The Senses as Doorways to Lost Memories*. Translated by Julian Ross, Oxford UP, 2014.

Willis, Paul. "The Golden Age." *On Record: Rock, Pop, and the Written Word*, edited by Simon Frith & Andrew Goodwin, Routledge, 1990, pp. 43-55.

Willman, Chris. "Grammy Winner Elvis Costello Says 'It Was More Punk' to Give Best New Artist to a Taste of Honey in 1979," *Variety*, 27 Jan. 2020, variety.com/2020/music/news/elvis-costello-grammy-winner-look-now-taste-of-honey-1203482677/

Wordsworth, William. "Lines Composed a Few Miles above Tintern Abbey." *Selected Poems and Prefaces*, edited by Jack Stillinger, Houghton Mifflin, 1965, pp. 108-111.

Zollo, Paul. "Stephen Stills: The One You're With." *More Songwriters on Songwriting*. De Capo Press, 2016, pp. 215-232.

About the Author

Chris Forhan is the author of the memoir *My Father Before Me* (Scribner, 2016) as well as three books of poetry: *Black Leapt In* (Barrow Street, 2009), winner of the Barrow Street Press Poetry Prize; *The Actual Moon, The Actual Stars* (Northeastern UP, 2003), winner of the Morse Poetry Prize and a Washington State Book Award; and *Forgive Us Our Happiness* (UP New England, 1999), winner of the Bakeless Prize. He is also the author of three chapbooks, *Ransack and Dance, x,* and *Crumbs of Bread,* and his poems have appeared in *Poetry, Paris Review, Ploughshares, New England Review, Parnassus, Georgia Review, Field, Gettysburg Review,* and other magazines, as well as in *The Best American Poetry.* He has won a National Endowment for the Arts Fellowship and three Pushcart Prizes, has earned a "Discover Great New Writers" selection from Barnes and Noble, and has been a resident at Yaddo and a fellow at Bread Loaf. He was born and raised in Seattle and lives with his wife, the poet Alessandra Lynch, and their two sons, Milo and Oliver, in Indianapolis, where he teaches at Butler University.